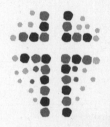

Aaron,

I loved this book! So, hopefully you will too :) Excited to see where God takes us when we both follow Him! Happy Graduation! :)

♥ Tara

A CALL TO DIE. A CALL TO LIVE.

FOLLOW ME

DAVID PLATT

INTRODUCTION BY
FRANCIS CHAN

TYNDALE HOUSE PUBLISHERS, INC., CAROL STREAM, ILLINOIS

Visit Tyndale online at www.tyndale.com.

TYNDALE and Tyndale's quill logo are registered trademarks of Tyndale House Publishers, Inc.

Follow Me: A Call to Die. A Call to Live.

Designed by Jennifer Ghionzoli

Published in association with Yates & Yates (www.yates2.com).

ISBN 978-1-4143-7328-7   Softcover
ISBN 978-1-4143-7676-9   Large Print edition

Printed in the United States of America

19   18   17   16   15   14   13

7   6   5   4   3   2   1

The author's royalties from this book will go toward promoting the glory of Christ in all nations.

To Caleb, Joshua, Mara Ruth, and Isaiah . . .
More than anything else, I pray that each of
you will find your life in his death.

CONTENTS

• ° •

INTRODUCTION

MY PERSONAL JOURNEY

I did what everyone expected me to do. I planted a megachurch. I wrote a bestseller. I started a college, planted other churches, and spoke at conferences. But there was a big problem: I lacked peace. Based on what I read in the Word, there were too many inconsistencies. My lifestyle did not resemble the life of Jesus, and the church I read about in Acts seemed so foreign. I realize that Jesus lived in a different culture and that Acts was written about a unique time in history, but I am convinced that certain qualities should always be true of Christians and the church.

It was no surprise to my wife, Lisa, and me when we sensed the Lord leading us on a new adventure. After seventeen years of fruitful ministry in one city (our entire married life), we left some deep and irreplaceable friendships to enter the unknown. I don't recommend this to everyone. It is not God's plan for every person, but it was for us. Simi Valley no longer seemed like the place I was most needed for the spread of the gospel. That was enough for us. Shouldn't all of our decisions be based upon what is going to have the greatest impact for God's Kingdom?

I wrestled with the number of Bible-teaching churches in this small city. I struggled with having so many godly leaders in one church while other cities were lacking or completely overlooked. I was frustrated with my own inability to motivate people to structure their lives around disciple making. I could fill a room and preach a sermon, but I couldn't figure out how to compel the people to leave that room and actually make disciples. I could generate excitement, but not urgency. I knew Jesus wanted more for his church, but I didn't know exactly what, and I didn't know how to lead them there.

Looking back, I can see now that part of the problem was my example. We all know that it's difficult to teach our children to do something we are not modeling. I told people to make disciples while I spent my days dealing with problems and preparing sermons. I wanted the people to share their faith regularly even though I rarely did. I expected the church to live adventurously while I continued my routine.

Peace began flooding back to me when we sold our home, packed up the family, and headed for Asia. It's weird how uncertainty can actually bring peace while ease causes the opposite. We chose Asia because I heard so many stories about the faith of the believers there. I wanted to witness it firsthand and see if the Lord was calling me there. I thought I might fit in better overseas and be better utilized in a different culture. Regardless of the outcome, I was enjoying the process. It was a rush to be in foreign countries, praying with my family, and asking the Lord if he wanted us to stay. In many ways, it was a dream come true.

We learned a lot while we were in Asia, but I concluded that the Lord was not done with me in America. He wanted me to take what I had learned from the believers in China and India and apply it here in the States. Their passion and commitment reminded me of what I read in the Scriptures. They displayed New Testament Christianity in the twenty-first century. They showed how rapidly and effectively the gospel spreads when every believer makes disciples. I am convinced that their mentality and approach to church could be just as transformative in the States. But we would have to be willing.

So I'm back in the United States. I'm still unsure of God's overarching plan for me, but this has been one of the best seasons of my life. I spend most of my days in San Francisco with a group of friends who go from person to person, explaining the gospel to anyone who will listen. A church is developing where disciple making is central and unity is natural. We are quickly becoming a family. I have found that it is much easier to put aside disagreements with fellow soldiers who sacrifice to make disciples.

I have more peace about my pursuit of those who don't know Jesus (I'm less of a coward). I have seen tremendous spiritual growth in my children. I love watching them share their faith and hearing their excitement when they witness the supernatural. We have seen God answer many prayers supernaturally. We are less attached to the world and more focused on eternity. My wife and kids are becoming more like Jesus, and our lifestyles more congruent with the New Testament. As my sixteen-year-old put it after our first outreach, "It felt like we popped out of the Bible."

The church I am a part of is a work in progress, but it is headed in the right direction. It is becoming more and more like what I see in Scripture. There is life, love, sacrifice, commitment, and power. Much of my time is spent actually making disciples, and ministry is making sense within this framework.

For too long, I wrestled with the simple math. Things made sense when I managed fifty people and saw them reach out to five hundred. I felt like a successful manager. It made sense when I was entrusted with five hundred workers and saw them reach five thousand. But that's when the system crashed. I was given the huge responsibility of leading five thousand workers. That's a massive workforce! And while we saw some good things happen, I didn't keep the workers multiplying. The growth we saw did not make sense considering the size of the army. The math didn't add up. I was wasting resources.

The issue is not about having a small church or a big one. It is about how to keep the great commission at the forefront of every believer's mind. It is about helping the church go beyond "come and listen" to "go and tell." It is about believers experiencing real life and about the church of Jesus shining brightly.

MAKING EVERY DAY A MISSION TRIP

Have you ever been on a short-term mission trip? Wasn't it fascinating? For a few days you explored a foreign country with a group of believers and were focused on ministry. You laughed together as you ate strange foods and tried to speak the language. You wept as you witnessed extreme poverty. Maybe you even suffered through sickness, harsh conditions, or actual persecution.

As nice as it was to return to the comforts of home, there was also a letdown. You were back in the "real world." There was a peace you felt when you did Kingdom work, and then it faded. You returned to a routine in which you felt like much of what you do has no eternal value. But what if it was possible to prolong the excitement and peace? What if life could be one continuous mission trip? Is this even possible in the "real world"?

Not only is it possible, it is what God wants for us.

Do you remember the verse that many of us heard when we first believed? "The thief comes only to steal and kill and destroy. I came that they may have life and have it abundantly."[1]

The life God has for us is one of abundance. It is meant to be full, not repetitive. He wants us doing things that have eternal impact. He wants us busy expanding his Kingdom in one way or another, today and every day. This doesn't mean that every Christian should quit his or her job and move to a foreign country. But it does mean that we need to figure out how to make each day count for his purposes.

Paul said it like this: "No soldier gets entangled in civilian pursuits, since his aim is to please the one who enlisted him."[2]

Don't most of us do the opposite? We busy ourselves with "civilian pursuits" and occasionally jump into the battle when we feel compelled. Kingdom service is something we visit on a mission trip, day of service, or prayer meeting. Being entangled in the civilian lifestyle has become the accepted norm. It is even applauded so long as we can point to some occasional Kingdom activity. But doesn't Scripture tell us to live differently? And wouldn't your life be more "abundant" if you could figure out a way to be on the battlefield every day?

You may be looking at your life and assuming you have no

options. Isn't a person with bills, family, and responsibilities destined to be "entangled in civilian pursuits"?

Absolutely not. You and I were made for more.

WHERE THERE'S A COMMAND, THERE'S A WAY

Jesus would never give us an impossible command. Whenever he allows temptation, he provides a way of escape.[3] Whenever he gives us a task, he provides us with the power to accomplish it.[4] Giving us a command without also giving us the power to obey would make life frustrating, not *abundant*.

Completing tasks with excellence is one of the joys of life. We love it when we ace a test after studying like crazy or win a game after competing with all we have. We are envious when we watch an Olympic athlete win the gold after years of dedication. We love seeing hard work pay off.

God created us to do good works.[5] And here's the crazy thing: not only does God give us commands, not only does he give us power to obey those commands, but he also rewards us when we've done what he commanded us! That is the abundant life.

Probably the most memorable task he gave was in Matthew 28. It stands out because of the dramatic fashion in which he gave it. *He rose from the grave*, and then prefaced his command with the words, "All authority in heaven and on earth has been given to me." No one in his right mind would ignore the next words out of Jesus' mouth:

> Go therefore and make disciples of all nations, baptizing
> them in the name of the Father and of the Son and of

the Holy Spirit, teaching them to observe all that I have commanded you.[6]

Jesus wanted followers from every nation on earth, so he commanded his disciples to reach them and train them. And that's exactly what they did—but this work is still not finished. He expects us to follow in their footsteps and structure our lives so that our actions revolve around completing this mission.

The church began in Acts 2 when three thousand people were converted. By AD 100, estimates claim twenty-five thousand followers. By AD 350, estimates claim over thirty *million* followers.[7]

How could the church grow at this incredible rate, especially under persecution? The early followers saw their obligation to make disciples. We see the same mind-set with the church in China. So we shouldn't be surprised to learn that the results are also the same. China claimed one million followers in 1950. In 1992, the State Statistical Bureau of China indicated that there were seventy-five million Christians.[8] Is it so impossible to believe that Christians could have this same disciple-making mind-set and experience the same type of revival here in America?

Ultimately, it doesn't matter if you like this strategy or not. We don't really have an option. That is the point of a command.

You take a big chance if you ignore an assignment given to you from your boss at work. Most of us would never consider it. So how can we ignore the King of the universe who will one day return as Judge?

The command can feel overwhelming. Many already live busy lives and at times feel like they are on the brink of meltdown. How could Jesus, who said, "My yoke is easy and my burden is light,"[9] throw such an enormous burden upon us? The answer is to consider who you are "yoked"—or joined together—with. Picture the imagery of two oxen placed under one yoke. Now picture yourself yoked with Jesus! Who wouldn't want that? Isn't this more of an honor than a burden?

Jesus ends his command by comforting us: "And behold, I am with you always, to the end of the age."[10] He promises to accompany his workers until his work is done. This is what gives us peace, confidence, and even anticipation.

MISSING OUT?

When people say that they don't "feel close to Jesus," I ask them if they are making disciples. After all, his promise to be with us is directly tied to his command to make disciples. While every Christian wants to experience the power of the Holy Spirit, we often forget that the Spirit's power is given for the purpose of being his witnesses.[11] Experiencing God, which is the longing of every true believer, happens when we are being his witnesses and making disciples.

There's nothing more exciting than experiencing the power of God firsthand. We would all love to stand with Elijah as he called down fire from heaven or to walk with Daniel through a den of lions or to see Peter and John tell a crippled man to stand up and walk. But these miracles happened when God's servants were being his witnesses in dangerous situations. We miss out on seeing the Spirit's power when we refuse to live by faith. We miss out on experiencing Christ when we don't speak up for him.

What's most tragic is that we could be experiencing God but instead we are experiencing guilt! Our fear of following him into a life spent making disciples leaves us feeling disappointed in ourselves.

Don't you struggle with this kind of guilt?

You read the Bible and believe that Jesus is the only way to heaven. You fear that those who die apart from Christ face a horrifying future. Yet for whatever reason, you've made little effort to warn your family and friends. You have neighbors, coworkers, and others you pass by daily without saying a word to them about Jesus.

You look at your life and think, *This doesn't make sense! Either I don't really believe the Bible, or I'm extremely unloving. I'm more concerned about being rejected than I am about someone else's eternal destiny.*

Much of my life was plagued with guilt because I knew that my actions did not make sense in light of my beliefs.

God doesn't want us to live this way. He wants us free from guilt and full of life. But the solution is not to ignore our guilt, nor is it to justify our actions, comparing ourselves to others who are just as complacent. The answer is repentance. Change.

I see a trend in many churches where people are beginning to *enjoy* convicting sermons. They walk out feeling broken over their sin. The distorted part is that they can begin to feel *victorious in their sadness*. They boast, "I just heard the most convicting message, and it ruined me!" The focus is on the conviction itself and not the change it is meant to produce—change that doesn't necessarily follow when we stay focused on conviction. Guilt is not always a good thing. It is only good if it leads us past sorrow to the joy of repentance.

Remember that the rich young ruler walked away sad, while Zacchaeus (who was also rich) leaped out of a tree with excitement.[12] The difference between the two was repentance. The rich ruler was sad because he wasn't ready to let go. Zacchaeus let go of his pride and possessions to joyfully follow Jesus. This is what Christ wants for us.

It's time we trade our guilt and sorrow for the joy of the Lord. No regrets.

> For godly grief produces a repentance that leads to salvation without regret, whereas worldly grief produces death.[13]

FINISH STRONG

We've all made our mistakes, and dwelling in the past can destroy us. The solution is to make the most of the time we have left on this earth.

Paul made an amazing statement in Acts 20:

> I testify to you this day that I am innocent of the blood of all, for I did not shrink from declaring to you the whole counsel of God.[14]

Wouldn't you love to be able to say that! Paul could live with himself because he didn't back down. He said all that he was supposed to say! When his life was nearly over, he could say with integrity,

> The time of my departure has come. I have fought the good fight, I have finished the race, I have kept the

faith. Henceforth there is laid up for me the crown of righteousness, which the Lord, the righteous judge, will award to me on that Day, and not only to me but also to all who have loved his appearing.[15]

Like the Olympic athlete waiting to receive his gold medal, Paul's work was done. Now he was just waiting for his "crown." Paul completed the assignment he was given. Much like Jesus, who said, "I . . . accomplished the work that you gave me to do."[16]

Right now, imagine yourself saying those words to God!

Could there be anything better than approaching his throne, knowing that you finished what he asked of you? It's hard to believe that we could actually hear the voice of Jesus acknowledging *us* to the Father, but he promised it:

Everyone who acknowledges me before men, I also will acknowledge before my Father who is in heaven, but whoever denies me before men, I also will deny before my Father who is in heaven.[17]

It is time for all of us to stop denying him. We have missed out on experiencing his presence and power for too long. It is time to move past our fears and get to work. The book you hold in your hands is all about living your life with peace as a disciple of Jesus and ending your life with confidence as you make disciples of Jesus. This book is about the exhilarating journey of eternal life that awaits every person who truly responds to Jesus' simple invitation: "Follow me."

I first met David Platt backstage at a conference where we were both preaching in early 2011. As we looked out over the crowd of thousands, we talked about how amazing it would be if we could somehow encourage and equip this crowd to make disciples. We both agreed that a book should be written to explain the need and hopefully mobilize the masses. I am so grateful that this book has been written.

These are exciting times. There are thousands in America who see the problems in the church and are committed to bringing change. True followers are rising up who refuse to be spectators or consumers. Jesus told us to go and make disciples, so we refuse to sit and make excuses.

I pray that you will join the growing number of believers who are committed to making disciples, who actually make disciples, who tirelessly make disciples until every nation has had the opportunity to follow Jesus.

What other option do we have?

Francis Chan

CHAPTER 1

UNCONVERTED BELIEVERS

IMAGINE A WOMAN NAMED AYAN.

Ayan is part of a people who pride themselves on being 100 percent Muslim. To belong to Ayan's tribe is to be Muslim. Ayan's personal identity, familial honor, relational standing, and social status are all inextricably intertwined with Islam. Simply put, if Ayan ever leaves her faith, she will immediately lose her life. If Ayan's family ever finds out that she is no longer a Muslim, they will slit her throat without question or hesitation.

Now imagine having a conversation with Ayan about Jesus. You start by telling her how God loves her so much that he sent his only Son to die on the cross for her sins as her Savior. As you speak, you can sense her heart softening toward what you are saying. At the same time, though, you can feel her spirit trembling as she contemplates what it would cost for her to follow Christ. With fear in her eyes and faith in her heart, she asks, "How do I become a Christian?"

You have two options in your response to Ayan. You can tell her how easy it is to become a Christian. If Ayan will simply assent to certain truths and repeat a particular prayer, she can be saved. That's all it takes.

Your second option is to tell Ayan the truth. You can tell Ayan that in the gospel, God is calling her to die.

Literally.

To die to her life.

To die to her family.

To die to her friends.

To die to her future.

And in dying, to live. To live in Jesus. To live as part of a global family that includes every tribe. To live with friends who span every age. To live in a future where joy will last forever.

Ayan is not imaginary. She is a real woman I met who made a real choice to become a Christian—to die to herself and to live in Christ, no matter what it cost her. Because of her decision, she was forced to flee her family and became isolated from her friends. Yet she is now working strategically and sacrificially for the spread of the gospel among her people. The risk is high as every day she dies to herself all over again in order to live in Christ.

Ayan's story is a clear reminder that the initial call to Christ is an inevitable call to die. Such a call has been clear since the beginning of Christianity. Four fishermen stood by a sea in the first century when Jesus approached them. "Follow me," he said, "and I will make you fishers of men."[1] With that, Jesus beckoned these men to leave behind their professions, possessions, dreams, ambitions, family, friends, safety, and security. He bid them to abandon everything. "If anyone is going to follow me, he must deny himself," Jesus would say repeatedly. In a world where everything revolves around self—protect yourself, promote yourself, preserve yourself, entertain yourself, comfort yourself, take care of yourself—Jesus said, "Slay yourself." And that's exactly what happened. According to Scripture and tradition, these four fishermen paid a steep price for following Jesus. Peter was crucified upside down, Andrew was crucified in Greece, James was beheaded, and John was exiled.

Yet they believed it was worth the cost. In Jesus, these men found someone worth losing everything for. In Christ, they encountered a love that surpassed comprehension, a satisfaction that superseded circumstances, and a purpose that transcended every other possible pursuit in this world. They eagerly, willingly, and gladly lost their lives in order to know, follow, and proclaim him. In the footsteps of Jesus, these first disciples discovered a path worth giving their lives to tread.

Two thousand years later, I wonder how far we have wandered from this path. Somewhere along the way, amid varying cultural tides and popular church trends, it seems that we have minimized Jesus' summons to total abandonment. Churches are filled with supposed Christians who seem content to have casual association with Christ while giving nominal adherence to Christianity. Scores of men, women, and children have been told that becoming a follower of Jesus simply involves acknowledging certain facts or saying certain words. But this is not true. Disciples like Peter, Andrew, James, John, and Ayan show us that the call to follow Jesus is not simply an invitation to pray a prayer; it's a summons to lose our lives.

Why, then, would we think that becoming a Christian means anything less for us? And why would we *not* want to die to ourselves in order to live in Christ? Yes, there is a cost that accompanies stepping out of casual, comfortable, cultural Christianity, but it is worth it. More aptly put, *he* is worth it. Jesus is worthy of far more than intellectual belief, and there is so much more to following him than monotonous spirituality. There is indescribable joy to be found, deep satisfaction to be felt, and an eternal purpose to be fulfilled in dying to ourselves and living for him.

That's why I've written this book. In a previous book, *Radical*, I sought to expose values and ideas that are common in our culture (and in the church) yet antithetical to the gospel. My aim was to consider the thoughts and things of this world that we must let go of in order to follow Jesus. The purpose of this book, then, is to take the next step. I want to move from *what* we let go of to *whom* we hold on to. I want to explore not only the gravity of what we must forsake in this world, but also the greatness of the one we follow in this world. I want to expose what it means to die to ourselves and to live in Christ.

I invite you to join me on this journey in the pages ahead. Along the way, I want to pose some particular questions about common phrases in contemporary Christianity. My goal in considering these questions is not to correct anyone who has ever used certain words, but simply to uncover potential dangers hiding behind popular clichés. Even as I ask such questions, I don't assume to have all the answers, and I don't claim to understand everything that following Jesus entails. But in a day when the basics of becoming and being a Christian are so maligned by the culture and misunderstood in the church, I do know that there is more to Jesus than the routine religion we are tempted to settle for at every turn. And I am convinced that when we take a serious look at what Jesus really meant when he said, "Follow me," we will discover that there is far more pleasure to be experienced in him, indescribably greater power to be realized with him, and a much higher purpose to be accomplished for him than anything else this world has to offer. And as a result, we will all—every single Christian—eagerly, willingly, and gladly lose our lives to know and proclaim Christ, for this is simply what it means to follow him.

PRAY THIS PRAYER

I have a friend—let's call him John—whose first exposure to the concept of hell was during an episode of *Tom and Jerry* when he was young. During one particularly vivid scene, Tom was sent to hell for something bad he had done to Jerry. What was intended to be a humorous cartoon scared John to death, and he later found himself at church talking with an older man about what he had seen.

The church man looked at John and said, "Well, *you* don't want to go to hell, do you?"

"No," he responded.

"Okay, then," the man said, "pray this prayer after me. Dear Jesus . . ."

John paused. After an awkward silence, he realized he was supposed to repeat after the man, and so he hesitantly responded, "Dear Jesus . . ."

"I know I'm a sinner, and I know Jesus died on a cross for my sins," the man said.

John followed suit.

"I ask you to come into my heart and to save me from my sin," the man said.

Again, John echoed what he had heard.

"Amen," the man concluded.

Then the man looked at John and said, "Son, you are saved from your sins, and you don't ever have to worry about hell again."

Surely what that man told my friend in church that day was not true. Surely this is not what it means to respond to Jesus' invitation to follow him. Yet this story represents deception that has spread like wildfire across the contemporary Christian landscape.

Just ask Jesus into your heart.

Simply invite Christ into your life.

Repeat this prayer after me, and you will be saved.

Should it alarm us that the Bible never mentions such a prayer? Should it concern us that nowhere in Scripture is anyone ever told to "ask Jesus into their heart" or to "invite Christ into their life"? Yet this is exactly what multitudes of professing Christians have been encouraged to do, and they've been assured that as long as they said certain words, recited a particular prayer, raised their hand, checked a box, signed a card, or walked an aisle, they are Christians and their salvation is eternally secure.

It's not true. With good intentions and sincere desires to reach as many people as possible for Jesus, we have subtly and deceptively minimized the magnitude of what it means to follow him. We've replaced challenging words from Christ with trite phrases in the church. We've taken the lifeblood out of Christianity and put Kool-Aid in its place so that it tastes better to the crowds, and the consequences are catastrophic. Multitudes of men and women at this moment think that they are saved from their sins when they are not. Scores of people around the world culturally think that they are Christians when biblically they are not.

"I NEVER KNEW YOU"

Is that possible? Is it possible for you or me to profess to be a Christian and yet not know Christ? Absolutely. And according to Jesus, it's actually *probable*.

Do you remember his words near the conclusion of his most famous sermon? Surrounded by people who are actually referred to as disciples, Jesus said,

> Not everyone who says to me, "Lord, Lord," will enter
> the kingdom of heaven, but only he who does the will
> of my Father who is in heaven. Many will say to me on
> that day, "Lord, Lord, did we not prophesy in your name,
> and in your name drive out demons and perform many
> miracles?" Then I will tell them plainly, "I never knew
> you. Away from me, you evildoers!"[2]

These are some of the most frightening words in all the Bible. As a pastor, I stay awake some nights haunted by the thought that *many* people sitting in church on Sunday may be surprised one day to stand before Jesus and hear him say to them, "I never knew you; away from me!"

We are all prone to spiritual deception—every single one of us. When Jesus says these words in Matthew 7, he's not talking about irreligious atheists, agnostics, pagans, and heretics. He's talking about good, religious people—men and women associated with Jesus who assume that their eternity is safe and will one day be shocked to find that it is not. Though they professed belief in Jesus and even did all kinds of work in his name, they never truly knew him.

Such deception was probable among first-century crowds and is probable in twenty-first-century churches. When I read Matthew 7, I think of Tom, a successful businessman in Birmingham who started attending the church I pastor. Tom has spent his entire life in church. He has served on just about every committee that any church has ever created. One of the pastors from Tom's former church even called one of our pastors to tell us what a great guy Tom is and how helpful Tom would be as a member in our church.

The only problem was that although he had served in the church for more than fifty years, Tom had never truly become a follower of Jesus. "For all those years I sat in the seats of churches thinking I knew Christ when I didn't," Tom said.

Jordan is a college student in our church with a similar story. Listen to her journey in her own words:

> I prayed to ask Jesus into my heart at the age of five. This prayer temporarily served as a "Get Out of Hell Free" card

while I continued to walk in sin. I looked better than all the other students in my youth group, so this served to validate my faith. If this validation was not enough, my parents, pastors, and friends told me I was a "Christian" whenever I questioned my faith because I had prayed that prayer and I looked nice on the outside, so they knew for sure I was "in."

But my heart was still not open to understanding grace. It was obvious that the prayer I prayed before was probably not going to cut it. So what did I do? I did what anybody would do who was not yet willing to admit their total brokenness and depravity before a holy God: I "rededicated" my life to Christ (a term that was not coined in Scripture, I assure you).

Yet I was still dead in my sin and not repentant. I still thought my good works committed in the past and those I would continue to do in the future counted for something. I could save myself; I was sure of it. I led Bible studies and went on mission trips, but none of that mattered. I was still by nature a child of wrath.

During my freshman year of college, I was finally confronted with the extreme tension that rested between my sinful self and God's holy nature. For the first time, I understood that the point of the cross was to justify the wrath of God that should have been directed toward me. I fell on my knees in fear and trembling and adoration and tears and confessed my need for Jesus more than I needed anything else in the world. Now I am pleased to confess that "I have been crucified with Christ. It is no longer I who live, but Christ who lives in me."[3]

After years in the church, Jordan underwent a massive transformation in her life from knowing *about* Jesus to living *in* Jesus. She went from working for Jesus in an attempt to earn God's favor to walking with Jesus out of the overflow of faith.

I don't think Tom's and Jordan's stories are unique. I believe they express a pandemic problem across contemporary Christianity. Masses of men, women, and children around the world just like Tom and Jordan are sitting comfortably under the banner of Christianity but have never counted the cost of following Christ.

THE HARD ROAD

This is why Jesus' words in Matthew 7 are so critical for us to hear. He exposes our dangerous tendency to gravitate toward that which is easy and popular. Hear his warning: "Enter by the narrow gate. For the gate is wide and the way is easy that leads to destruction, and those who enter by it are many. For the gate is narrow and the way is hard that leads to life, and those who find it are few."[4] In other words, there is a broad religious road that is inviting and inclusive. This nice, comfortable, ever-so-crowded path is attractive and accommodating. The only thing that's required of you is a one-time decision for Christ, and you don't have to worry about his commands, his standards, or his glory after making that decision. You now have a ticket to heaven, and your sin, whether manifested in self-righteousness or self-indulgence, will be tolerated along the way.

But this is not the way of Jesus. He beckons us down a hard road, and the word Jesus uses for "hard" is associated in other parts of the Bible with pain, pressure, tribulation, and persecution. The way of Jesus is hard to follow, and it's hated by many.

Just a few chapters after these words in Matthew 7, Jesus told his disciples that they would be beaten, betrayed, mistreated, isolated, and killed for following him. "Be on your guard," Jesus said, "[for] they will hand you over to the local councils and flog you in their synagogues. On my account you will be brought before governors and kings. . . . Brother will betray brother to death, and a father his child. . . . All men will hate you because of me."[5]

On another occasion, right after Jesus commended Peter for his confession of faith in him as "the Christ, the Son of the living God," Jesus rebuked Peter for missing the magnitude of what this means. Like many people today, Peter wanted a Christ without a cross and a Savior without any suffering. So Jesus looked at Peter and the other disciples and said, "If anyone would come after me, he must deny himself and take up his cross and follow me. For whoever wants to save his life will lose it, but whoever loses his life for me will find it."[6]

Shortly before Jesus went to the cross, he told his disciples, "You will be handed over to be persecuted and put to death, and you will be hated by all nations because of me."[7] In each of these passages in the book of Matthew, the call to die is clear. The road that leads to heaven is risky, lonely, and costly in this world, and few are willing to pay the price. Following Jesus involves losing your life—and finding new life in him.

Not long ago, I was serving in North Africa alongside persecuted brothers and sisters. I talked with one man who just months before had his leg shattered in a church bombing. I talked with a pastor who shared with me how women in his church were being kidnapped, abused, and raped for being Christians. I had dinner in a family's house where just two blocks away a follower of Jesus had been stabbed in the heart and killed.

I heard the story of three Christians who had moved overseas from the United States to work at a hospital in this region. In a move that most people in the world (and many people in the church) would call foolish and unwise, they had left behind their comforts, careers, family, friends, safety, and security to share the goodness and grace of Christ in a land where it is forbidden to become a Christian. Day after day in that hospital, they met physical needs while sharing spiritual truth.

They knew there was opposition to their work, but nothing could have prepared them for the day when a man walked into their hospital with a fake bandage on his hand and a blanket bundled to look like a baby. He entered the office area and immediately unwrapped the blanket to reveal a loaded rifle. Beginning in the office and working his way through the rest of the clinic, he shot and killed all three of these brothers and sisters.

During my time in this country, the ten-year anniversary of that shooting was approaching, so we set aside time to remember these three Christians. Our commemoration happened to be near the grave of Oswald Chambers. Consequently, we thought it appropriate to read from Chambers's well-known devotional, *My Utmost for His Highest*, on that particular day. It was as if his words were written for the occasion. Chambers says:

Suppose God tells you to do something that is an enormous test of your common sense, totally going against it. What will you do? Will you hold back? If you get into the habit of doing something physically, you will do it every time you are tested until you break the habit through sheer determination. And the same is true spiritually. Again and again you will come right up to what Jesus wants, but every time you will turn back at the true point of testing, until you are determined to abandon yourself to God in total surrender. . . .

Jesus Christ demands the same unrestrained, adventurous spirit in those who have placed their trust in Him. . . . If a person is ever going to do anything worthwhile, there will be times when he must risk everything by his leap in the dark. In the spiritual realm, Jesus Christ demands that you risk everything you hold on to or believe through common sense, and leap by faith into what He says. Once you obey, you will immediately find that what He says is as solidly consistent as common sense.

By the test of common sense, Jesus Christ's statements may seem mad, but when you test them by the trial of faith, your findings will fill your spirit with the awesome fact that they are the very words of God. Trust completely in God, and when He brings you to a new opportunity of adventure, offering it to you, see that you take it. We act like pagans in a crisis—only one out of an entire crowd is daring enough to invest his faith in the character of God.[8]

Chambers's words, viewed through the lens of these three martyrs' lives, challenge us to consider the seeming madness of Jesus' words:

> If anyone comes to me and does not hate his father and mother, his wife and children, his brothers and sisters— yes, even his own life—he cannot be my disciple. And anyone who does not carry his cross and follow me cannot be my disciple. . . . Any of you who does not give up everything he has cannot be my disciple.[9]

To everyone else in the world, these words seem crazy. But to every Christian, these words are life. For the few who choose to abandon themselves to the will of God and put their trust in the character of God, following Jesus wherever he leads, no matter the cost, is the only thing that makes sense.

WHAT ABOUT BELIEF?

Amid this emphasis on the cost of following Jesus, you might wonder about passages in the Bible where it seems that salvation involves simple belief. Jesus tells Nicodemus that "God so loved the world that he gave his one and only Son, that whoever *believes* in him shall not perish but have eternal life." Paul and Silas tell the Philippian jailer, "*Believe* in the Lord Jesus, and you will be saved." According to the book of Romans, "If you confess with your mouth, 'Jesus is Lord,' and *believe* in your heart that God raised him from the dead, you will be saved."[10] Based on these passages, you might conclude that believing in Jesus is all that's involved in becoming or being a Christian.

This is absolutely true, but we must consider context in order to understand what the Bible means by belief. When Jesus calls Nicodemus to believe in him, he is calling Nicodemus to be born again—to begin an entirely new life devoted to following him. Likewise, when the Philippian jailer believes in Christ, he knows that he is joining a community of Christians who are being beaten, flogged, and imprisoned for their faith. The cost of following Christ is clear. In the same way, Paul tells the Roman Christians that to believe in the saving resurrection of Jesus from the dead is to confess the sovereign lordship of Jesus over their lives.

In each of these verses (and scores of others like them), belief in Jesus for salvation involves far more than mere intellectual assent. After all, even demons "believe" that Jesus is the crucified and resurrected Son of God.[11] Such "belief" clearly doesn't save, yet such "belief" is common across the world today. Just about every intoxicated person I meet on the street says he "believes" in Jesus. Scores of people I meet around the world, including some Hindus, animists, and Muslims, profess some level of "belief" in Jesus. All kinds of halfhearted, world-loving church attenders confess "belief" in Christ.

We can all profess publicly belief that we don't possess personally, even (or should I say *especially*) in the church. Hear the shouts of the damned in Matthew 7 as they cry, "Lord, Lord!" Jesus replies to them, "Not everyone who says to me, 'Lord, Lord,' will enter the kingdom of heaven, but only he who does the will of my Father who is in heaven."[12] Clearly, people who claim to believe in Jesus are not assured eternity in heaven. On the contrary, only those who obey Jesus will enter his Kingdom.

As soon as I write that, you may perk up and ask, "David, did you just say that *works* are involved in our salvation?" In response to that question, I want to be clear: that is not what I am saying.

Instead, it's what *Jesus* is saying.

Now I want to be very careful here, because we could begin to twist the gospel into something it's not. Jesus is not saying that our works are the *basis* for our salvation. The grace of God is the *only* basis of our salvation—a truth we will explore further in the next chapter. But in our rush to defend grace, we cannot overlook the obvious in what Jesus is saying here (and in many other places as well): only those who are obedient to the words of Christ will enter the Kingdom of Christ. If our lives do not reflect the fruit of following Jesus, then we are foolish to think that we are actually followers of Jesus in the first place.

DANGEROUSLY DECEIVED

Consider a recent study which found that four out of five Americans identify themselves as Christians. In this group of self-proclaimed Christians, less than half of them are involved in church on a weekly basis. Less than half of them actually believe the Bible is accurate, and the overwhelming majority of them don't have a biblical view of the world around them.

The pollsters went even deeper, though, to identify men and women who are described as "born-again Christians" (as if there is any other kind). These are people who say they have made a personal commitment to Jesus and who believe they will go to heaven because they have accepted Jesus as their Savior. According to the research, almost half of Americans are "born-again Christians."

But out of this group of "born-again Christians," researchers found that their beliefs and lifestyles are virtually indistinguishable from the rest of the world around them. Many of these "born-again Christians" believe that their works can earn them a place in heaven, others think that Christians and Muslims worship the same God, some believe Jesus sinned while he was on earth, and an ever-increasing number of "born-again Christians" describe themselves as only marginally committed to Jesus.[13]

Many people have used this data to conclude that Christians are really not that different from the rest of the world. But I don't think this interpretation of the research is accurate. I think the one thing that is abundantly clear from these statistics is that there are a whole lot of people in the world who think they are Christians but are not. There are a whole lot of people who think that they've been born again, but they are dangerously deceived.

Imagine you and I set up a meeting for lunch at a restaurant, and you arrive before I do. You wait and wait and wait, but thirty minutes later, I still haven't arrived. When I finally show up, completely out of breath, I say to you, "I'm so sorry I'm late. When I was driving over here, my car had a flat tire, and I pulled over on the side of the interstate to fix it. While I was fixing it, I accidentally stepped into the road, and a Mack truck going about seventy miles per hour suddenly hit me head-on. It hurt, but I picked myself up, finished putting the spare tire on the car, and drove over here."

If this were the story I shared, you would know I was either deliberately lying or completely deceived. Why? Because if someone gets hit by a Mack truck going seventy miles per hour, that person is going to look *very* different than he did before![14]

In light of this, I feel like I'm on pretty safe ground in assuming that once people truly come face-to-face with Jesus, the God of the universe in the flesh, and Jesus reaches down into the depth of their hearts, saves their souls from the clutches of sin, and transforms their lives to follow him, they are going to look different. *Very* different. People who claim to be Christians while their lives look no different from the rest of the world are clearly not Christians.

Such deception is not just evident in the United States; it's prevalent around the world. As I was praying through the countries of the world recently, I came across Jamaica, a country that is supposedly almost 100 percent Christian. The prayer guide I use made this statement about Jamaica: "It enjoys one of the world's highest number of churches per square mile, but the majority of self-proclaimed Christians in Jamaica neither attend church nor lead a Christian life."[15] As I read this, my heart was overcome by the unavoidable conclusion that multitudes of men and women in Jamaica think they are Christians when they are not. They join scores of people in countries around the world who call themselves Christians yet don't follow Christ.

Spiritual deception is dangerous—and damning. Any one of us can fool ourselves. We are sinful creatures, biased in our own favor, prone to assume that we are something when we are not. The Bible says that the god of this world (Satan) is blinding the minds of unbelievers to keep them from knowing Christ.[16] Couldn't it be that one of the ways the devil is doing this is by deceiving people into believing they are Christians when they are not?

THE SIGNIFICANCE OF REPENTANCE

So how does a person truly become a follower of Jesus? What happens when the Mack truck of God's glory and grace collides with someone's life? The rest of this book is consumed with an answer to that question, but consider for a moment one word that summarizes Jesus' summons.

The very first word out of Jesus' mouth in his ministry in the New Testament is clear: repent.[17] It's the same word that John the Baptist proclaims in preparation for Jesus' coming.[18] This word is also the foundation for the first Christian sermon in the book of Acts. After Peter proclaims the good news of Christ's death for sin, the crowds ask him, "What shall we do?" Peter decidedly does not tell them to close their eyes, repeat after him, or raise their hands. Instead, Peter determinedly looks them right in their eyes and says, "Repent."[19]

Repentance is a rich biblical term that signifies an elemental transformation in someone's mind, heart, and life. When people repent, they turn from walking in one direction to running in the opposite direction. From that point forward, they think differently, believe differently, feel differently, love differently, and live differently.

When Jesus said, "Repent," he was speaking to people who were rebelling against God in their sin and relying on themselves for their salvation. Jesus' predominantly Jewish audience believed that their family heritage, social status, knowledge of specific rules, and obedience to certain regulations were sufficient to make them right before God.

Jesus' call to repentance, then, was a summons for them to renounce sin and all dependence on self for salvation. Only by turning from their sin and themselves and toward Jesus could they be saved.

Similarly, when Peter said, "Repent," he was speaking to crowds who not long before had crucified Jesus. In their sin, they had killed the Son of God and were now standing under the judgment of God. Peter's call to repentance was a cry for the crowds to confess their wickedness, turn from their ways, and trust in Jesus as Lord and Christ.

Fundamentally, then, repentance involves renouncing a former way of life in favor of a new way of life. God tells his people in the Old Testament, "Repent! Turn from your idols and renounce all your detestable practices!"[20] Similarly, in the New Testament, repentance requires turning from the idols of this world to a new object of worship.[21]

I remember a particular moment with a house church in Asia. We were meeting in a secret, isolated location on the outskirts of a remote rural village. The impoverished homes in this village were virtual warehouses for idols. Satanic superstition abounded as village residents were convinced that they needed a multiplicity of gods to protect and provide for them.

One woman in particular caught my attention during our meetings. She listened eagerly to everything I shared from God's Word, and it was evident that the Lord was drawing her to himself. At the end of the day, she expressed a desire to follow Jesus. We were thrilled.

The next day, this new sister in Christ came back and pulled the church's pastor and me aside. She told us that her home was full of false gods she had worshiped all her life and that she wanted to get rid of them. The other pastor and I accompanied her to her house, and I was overwhelmed by what I saw.

Inside the small, dark, two-room home, black and red posters of false gods covered the walls. Demonic-looking clay and wooden figurines were resting on the floor and sitting on tables everywhere we turned. In the middle of one room, a large idol was mounted against the wall with its foreboding face staring directly at us.

We immediately began taking down the posters and taking hold of the idols, praying aloud for this woman and for God's blessings on her home for his glory. We brought every one of the idols back to the house where we were meeting, and we lit a fire outside. That day, we began our time in the Word amid the smell of smoldering gods.

This scene is an illustration of what happens in every person's life when we repent of our sin, renounce ourselves, and run in faith to Christ. We humbly see and gladly sear the idols of this world that we have worshiped. We turn from them to trust in Jesus as the one who we now realize is exclusively worthy of our exaltation.

When that woman became a Christian, it was obvious that she could no longer bow at the feet of false gods in her home, and she needed to get rid of them. Similarly, I think of Vasu, an Indian brother who used to give offerings and present sacrifices daily before a multiplicity of Hindu gods. Upon becoming a follower of Jesus, Vasu began to turn away from these idols. Or I think of Gunadi, a man who used to be a devout Muslim but recently trusted in Christ as Savior and King. In repentance,

Gunadi turned aside from the teachings of Muhammad to follow in the footsteps of Jesus.

In circumstances like these, repentance seems clear and obvious. Christians from animistic, Hindu, or Muslim backgrounds must turn aside from false gods in order to follow Christ, and repentance is evident in the transformation of their lives. But what about people in a predominantly "Christian" setting who aren't bowing down before idols or offering sacrifices to false gods? What does repentance look like in their lives?

This question is extremely important, for it exposes a fundamental flaw in the way we often view ourselves. When we think of worshiping idols and false gods, we often picture Asian people buying carved images of wood, stone, or gold or African tribes performing ritualistic dances around burning sacrifices. But we don't consider the American man looking at pornographic pictures online or watching ungodly television shows and movies. We don't think about the American woman incessantly shopping for more possessions or obsessively consumed with the way she looks. We don't take into account men and women in the Western world constantly enamored with money and blindly engulfed in materialism. We hardly even think about our busy efforts to climb the corporate ladder, our incessant worship of sports, our temper when things don't go our way, our worries that things won't go our way, our overeating, our excesses, and all sorts of other worldly indulgences. Maybe most dangerous of all, we overlook the spiritual self-achievement and religious self-righteousness that prevent scores of us from ever recognizing our need for Christ. We can't fathom a Christian on the other side of the world believing that a wooden god can save them, but we have no problem believing that religion, money, possessions, food, fame, sex, sports, status, and success can satisfy us. Do we actually think that we have fewer idols to let go of in our repentance?

For every Christian in every culture, repentance is necessary. This doesn't mean that when people become Christians, they suddenly become perfect and never have any struggles with sin again.[22] But this does mean that when we become followers of Jesus, we make a decided break with an old way of living and take a decisive turn to a new way of life. We literally die to our sin and to ourselves—our self-centeredness, self-consumption, self-righteousness, self-indulgence, self-effort, and self-exaltation. In the words of Paul, we "have been crucified with Christ and [we] no longer live, but Christ lives in [us]."[23]

And as Christ begins to live in us, everything begins to change about us. Our minds change. For the first time, we realize who God is, what Jesus has done, and how much we need him. Our desires change. The things of this earth that we once loved we now hate, and the things of God that we once hated we now love. Our wills change. We go wherever Jesus says, we give whatever Jesus commands, and we sacrifice whatever it costs to spend our lives in uncompromising obedience to his Word. Our relationships change. We lay our lives down in love for one another in the church as together we spread the gospel to the world.

Ultimately, our reason for living changes. Possessions and position are no longer our priorities. Comfort and security are no longer our concerns. Safety is no longer our goal because self is no longer our god. We now want God's glory more than we want our own lives. The more we glorify him, the more we enjoy him, and the more we realize that this is what it means biblically to be a Christian.

THE JOURNEY BEGINS

In the pages ahead, we will explore this revolution that occurs when a person comes face-to-face with God in the flesh and he says, "Follow me." We will consider the magnitude of the "me" we are called to follow and marvel at the wonder of his mercy toward us. As we discover how God transforms disciples of Jesus from the inside out, we will see the Christian life not as organized duty but as overwhelming delight. We will debunk popular Christian slogans and politically correct positions that keep us from truly knowing and passionately proclaiming Christ. In the end, we will find ourselves joined with brothers and sisters around the world accomplishing a grand and global purpose that God set in motion before the world even began.

The journey begins, though, with truly understanding what it means to be a Christian. To say that you believe in Jesus apart from conversion in your life completely misses the essence of what it means to follow him. Do not be deceived. Your relationship with Jesus and your status before God are not based on a decision you made, a prayer you prayed, a card you signed, or a hand you raised however many years ago. And the Christian life does not ultimately begin with inviting Jesus to come into your heart. As we'll see in the next chapter, that invitation comes from him.

CHAPTER 2

THE GREAT INVITATION

THROUGHOUT SCRIPTURE, God uses the picture of adoption to describe his relationship with his people. This picture became all the more poignant for my wife, Heather, and me when we chose to adopt our first son.

We began the process by deciding on the place from which we might adopt. We put a map of the world on the table and we prayed, "Lord, direct us to the child that you desire for us." He led us to adopt internationally from the country of Kazakhstan. I barely knew Kazakhstan existed before this process, but after months of praying, we submitted our application to adopt a Kazakh child.

Shortly thereafter, I remember telling a woman that we were adopting a child internationally. She responded, "A real one?" I thought to myself, *What kind of question is that? No, we're going to adopt a plastic one and put it on our mantel to look at. Yes, we're adopting a real child!* Though I responded with more tenderness than I felt inside, the reality began to set in: we were going to be a real mommy and a real daddy for a real son or daughter who, at that moment, had no real family to care for him or her.

The process of international adoption can be long and in many ways grueling. Some have described it as a paperwork pregnancy. You virtually have to demonstrate to two governments that you are the ideal family. First, we had to undergo a home study, which was a bit of a challenge since our house had recently been submerged by Hurricane Katrina in New Orleans. Through the help of our family and various churches, we put together a makeshift apartment as fast as we could. A social worker visited us and asked questions about our lives, families, marriage, and parenting philosophy. As part of the home study, we had to be fingerprinted by what seemed like every type of government or civic organization in the United States.

Then Heather and I had to get a physical that would verify a clean bill of health for us as parents. We went to the doctor's office, and everything was going well until we got to the eye chart. I went first, and I still maintain that the lighting was dim in the hallway where we stood. With my hand over my right eye, I began reading the large letters, but before long I was struggling with the medium-sized letters. I started sweating, thinking, *I can't fail this eye exam and delay the adoption process.* The nurse knew I was not doing well, so she suggested I switch eyes. I took my hand off my right eye, only to find that in my nervousness I had been pressing down hard on that eye, and everything was blurry. I couldn't even read the top letters now. I was visibly flustered, and the nurse said, "Why don't you calm down, sir, move over, and let your wife go? Then you can try again."

"That sounds great," I said, stepping aside to regain my composure and refocus my vision. Once I was able to do that, and as Heather was still completing her exam, with both eyes open I looked down at the letters and memorized them. When it was my turn to try again, I stood confidently with one eye covered and read off every single letter. The nurse was pleased that I was now getting them correct, and I thought to myself, *Hey, if you want me to, I can do this with both eyes covered!*

With home studies, fingerprints, and physicals past us, we began the long, agonizing process of waiting. Every single day, we thought about our child, wondering if it would be a boy or a girl and longing for the day when we could hold that little one in our arms.

Finally, about a year later, I received an e-mail. It was a picture of a boy. Nine months old. Abandoned at birth. In need of a home, a mom, and a dad. I printed out the picture and ran to show it to Heather. We laughed, we cried, we rejoiced, we prayed, and within two weeks, we were on a plane, headed to Kazakhstan.

It was the day after Valentine's Day in 2007. Upon arrival in our son's city, we were immediately taken to his orphanage, where the director met us and escorted us into a small room. She shared all sorts of medical information with us about our son, and then it happened. A woman rounded the corner with a precious ten-month-old boy in her arms. Words really can't describe the immediate swell of emotion that filled the room. The woman handed him to us, and for the first time, Caleb Platt looked into the eyes of a mom and a dad.

For the next four weeks, we visited Caleb in his orphanage. We held him, fed him, sang to him, laughed with him, and crawled all over the floor with him until the day finally came for us to adopt him. We were instructed on what to wear, what to say, and what to expect when we stood before a Kazakh judge. Our hearts were pounding in that courtroom as the proceeding played out. After a number of questions and testimonies concerning Caleb's background, the judge pronounced, "I grant this application of adoption, and this child now belongs to David and Heather Platt." We left the room with tears streaming from our eyes, ready to pick up Caleb from his orphanage for the last time.

The parallels between Caleb's story and the gospel story are many, but I want to point out one that is particularly significant. Adoption like this begins with a parent's initiative, not a child's idea. Before Caleb was even born in Kazakhstan, he had a mom and a dad working to adopt him. While Caleb was lying alone at night in an orphanage in Kazakhstan, he had a mom and a dad planning to adopt him. And one day when Caleb was placed in the arms of his mom and dad, he had no idea all that had been done, completely apart from any initiative in him, to bring him to that point. It seems obvious, but it is especially important: this precious ten-month-old boy did not invite us to come to him in Kazakhstan to bring him into our family; he didn't even know to ask for such a thing. No, this orphaned child became our cherished son because of a love that was entirely beyond his imagination and completely outside of his control. He did not pursue us, for he was utterly unable to do so. Instead, we pursued him.

This is the heart of Christianity, and we are prone to miss it when we describe becoming a follower of Jesus as inviting him into our hearts. The reality of the gospel is that we do not become God's children ultimately because of initiative in us, and he does not provide salvation primarily because of an invitation from us. Instead, before we were ever born, God was working to adopt us. While we were lying alone in the depth of our sin, God was planning to save us. And the only way we can become part of the family of God is through a love entirely beyond our imagination and completely out of our control. Christianity does not begin with our pursuit of Christ, but with Christ's pursuit of us. Christianity does not start with an invitation we offer to Jesus, but with an invitation Jesus offers to us.

DEAD PEOPLE DON'T INVITE

Consider the biblical background leading up to that fateful day for those four fishermen who first heard Jesus' invitation to follow him. This story in the first book of the New Testament takes us all the way back to the first book of the Old Testament. There in Genesis, the first man and first woman sinned against God and were separated from his presence. Orphaned from their Creator as a result of their rebellion, the rest of the Old Testament tells the story of their sinful descendants.

Murder, wickedness, sexual immorality, and corruption soon saturate the pages of the Bible. Only six chapters in, it becomes clear that the inclination of every person's heart is consistently evil, beginning from childhood.[1] The judgment of God on the depravity of man is both dreadful and devastating as he floods the entire world and then destroys sinful cities.

A perusal through the pages of the Old Testament shows severe punishment toward sin and sinners alike:

- As fire from heaven rains down on Sodom and Gomorrah, God instructs Lot and his family to flee and not look back toward these cities. In disobedience, Lot's wife glances back and suddenly loses her life.[2]
- After fire falls on Mount Sinai in a display of God's glory, God gives his law and instructs his people to rest on the Sabbath. Not long thereafter, a man is caught picking up sticks on the Sabbath, and he is brought before the Lord for judgment. In response to this man's sin and disobedience, the Lord declares that he should be stoned to death.[3]
- The same fate befalls Achan and his family when they disobey God's command not to keep plunder from a battle.[4]
- Aaron's sons Nadab and Abihu offer unauthorized fire before the Lord in the Tabernacle, and they are immediately consumed.[5]
- Though commanded not to touch the Ark of the Covenant, Uzzah reaches out to keep it from falling, and he immediately dies.[6]

Many people read stories like these in the Old Testament and walk away confused. After all, isn't God a God of love? Aren't these punishments for sin a bit severe? Annihilated for looking backward? Stoned for picking up sticks? Consumed for one wrong offering and killed for one inadvertent touch?

Such questions, though honest, reveal a fundamental problem with our perspective. We naturally view sin through man-centered eyes. The reason we wonder if these punishments are overly harsh is because we cannot imagine ever responding this way if the offenses were against us. When people disobey us or do something we have asked them not to do, we don't conclude that they should die.

Yet the penalty for sin is not determined by our measure of it. Instead, the penalty for sin is determined by the magnitude of the one who is sinned against. If you sin against a log, you are not very guilty. On the other hand, if you sin against a man or a woman, then you are absolutely guilty. And ultimately, if you sin against an infinitely holy and eternal God, you are infinitely guilty and worthy of eternal punishment.

Azeem, an Arab follower of Jesus and a friend of mine, was sharing the gospel recently with a taxi driver in his country. The driver believed that he would pay for his sin for a little while in hell, but then he would surely go to heaven after that. After all, he hadn't done too many bad things.

So Azeem said to him, "If I slapped you in the face, what would you do to me?"

The driver replied, "I would throw you out of my taxi."

Azeem continued, "If I went up to a random guy on the street and slapped him in the face, what would he do to me?"

The driver said, "He would probably call his friends and beat you up."

Azeem asked, "What if I went up to a policeman and slapped him in the face? What would he do to me?"

The driver replied, "You would be beat up for sure, and then thrown into jail."

Finally, Azeem posed this question: "What if I went to the king of this country and slapped him in the face? What would happen to me then?"

The driver looked at Azeem and awkwardly laughed. He told Azeem, "You would die."

To this Azeem said, "So you see that the severity of sin's punishment is always a reflection of the position of the person who is sinned against." The driver thus realized that he had been severely underestimating the seriousness of his sin against God.

How about you? Have you underestimated the seriousness of your sin? The likelihood is that you may have been led to do so in the church. For far too long we have convinced one another that we are basically good people who have simply made some bad decisions. Whether we've lied or cheated or stolen or taken God's name in vain, we've all made mistakes. We just need to invite Jesus to come into our hearts, and he will forgive us of all these things.

But assuming that we can even make this kind of invitation shows that we don't grasp the gravity of our sinfulness. In our sin, we are utterly unable to call on Christ because we are totally consumed with running from God. At the core of who we are, we are enemies of God with no real desire for God. Sure, we'll take a quick fix for our sin when it's offered to us—tell us the prayer to pray or the words to say, and we'll do it. Yet deep down inside we're still controlled by sinful hearts that are looking for a way to save our skin while we live for ourselves.

Lest you think that I'm overstating our sinfulness, listen to the testimony of the Bible.

- In our sin, we have alienated ourselves from God and are hostile toward him.[7]
- We are slaves to our sin and dominated by Satan.[8]
- We love darkness and hate light.[9]
- We live in impurity and wickedness.[10]
- Our minds are depraved, blinded to truth by the god of this world.[11]
- Our desires are disordered, our hearts are sinful, and the wicked passions of our flesh wage war against our souls.[12]
- Our bodies are defiled. We are morally evil and spiritually sick.[13]

Hear Paul's humbling New Testament testimony as he summarizes Old Testament truth:

There is no one righteous, not even one;
 there is no one who understands,
 no one who seeks God.
All have turned away,
 they have together become worthless;
there is no one who does good,
 not even one.

Their throats are open graves;
    their tongues practice deceit.
The poison of vipers is on their lips.
    Their mouths are full of cursing and bitterness.
Their feet are swift to shed blood;
    ruin and misery mark their ways,
and the way of peace they do not know.
    There is no fear of God before their eyes.[14]

Do we realize all of this? Our problem is not simply that we have made some bad decisions. Our problem is not just that we've messed up. Our problem is that we are—at the very core of our being— rebels against God, and we are utterly unable to turn to him.

This is what the Bible means when it says we are dead in sin. When Paul wrote to the Ephesian Christians and said, "You were dead in your transgressions and sins, in which you used to live,"[15] he meant that they were *completely* dead. Not partially dead. Not almost dead. Not halfway dead. Not kind of dead. *Completely* dead.

So how can people who are dead invite someone else to give them life? Before you were born, did you invite your parents to have you? When a man's heart is flatlined, does he invite people to resuscitate him? No. All of these things are impossible for those who are dead. Similarly, inviting Jesus to come into your heart is impossible when you're dead in sin. In your death, you need someone else, completely outside of you, to call you to life and enable you to live.

GRACIOUS INITIATIVE

This is what God does in his grace, and it's precisely what we see all throughout the Bible. In the midst of massive evil, God calls Noah and saves him from the Flood. In the middle of pagan Ur, God calls idolatrous Abraham and invites him to become the father of a great nation. While his people work as slaves in Egypt, God calls the murderer Moses from Midian to lead them out of slavery. Upon their deliverance, God tells the people of Israel, whom he had called,

> The LORD did not set his affection on you and choose
> you because you were more numerous than other peoples,
> for you were the fewest of all peoples. But it was because
> the LORD loved you and kept the oath he swore to your
> forefathers that he brought you out with a mighty hand
> and redeemed you from the land of slavery, from the
> power of Pharaoh king of Egypt.[16]

God chose to set his love on the Israelites not because of any merit in them but solely because of mercy in him.

The trend continues. Despite the obvious qualifications of all of Jesse's other sons, God appoints the unlikely David to become the king of Israel. He calls prophets like Elijah, Elisha, Isaiah, and Ezekiel. God tells Jeremiah, "Before I formed you in the womb I knew you, before you were born I set you apart; I appointed you as a prophet to the nations."[17] From the mass of sinners throughout the Old Testament, God initiates relationships with men and women that they might be the recipients of his grace for the display of his glory.

Therefore, we are not surprised when we get to the book of Matthew and see four sinful Jewish men standing by the sea. There is nothing in them to draw Christ to them. Sometimes I hear sermons on Matthew 4:18-22 in which preachers talk about all the reasons why Jesus would choose these fishermen to be his disciples. "Fishermen have this or that skill and hold this or that perspective, which would be essential for disciples of Jesus," they say.

But such conjecture misses the whole point of the story. Jesus is not calling these disciples *because* of who they are, but *in spite* of who they are. They do not have many qualities in their favor. They are lower class, rural, uneducated Galileans. Likely not well respected, they are hardly the culturally elite. Moreover, their exceeding ignorance, narrow-minded ways, Jewish prejudices, and competitive pride make them the least spiritually qualified for the task to which Jesus is calling them.

But *that* is the point. These men decidedly do not warrant Jesus' pursuit. Yet he comes to them. He walks up to them in the middle of their work, and he invites them to follow him. Later he tells them, "You did not choose me, but I chose you and appointed you."[18] These men become disciples of Jesus *solely* because of the initiative—and invitation—of Christ.

This same story is shared by every man and woman who has followed Jesus since that day described in Matthew 4. No one has ever been saved from their sins because they have pursued Jesus. Everyone who has ever been saved from their sins knows that they have been pursued by Jesus—and their lives haven't been the same since.

THE GREAT INITIATOR

When we realize that Jesus is the one who takes the initiative and invites us to follow him, everything changes—on multiple levels.

First, our souls are struck by the greatness of the one who has called us. We are overwhelmed by the magnitude of the words *follow me* because we are awed by the majesty of the "me" who says them.

Consider the eye-opening, jaw-dropping portrait of Jesus that Matthew paints leading up to this initial encounter between Jesus and his first disciples.[19] Matthew describes Jesus as the Savior who came to deliver men and women from their sins. He tells us that Jesus is the Christ, the promised Messiah whom God's people for centuries had eagerly anticipated and anxiously awaited. In his description of the Virgin Birth, Matthew puts Jesus' full humanity and full deity on display, making it clear that Jesus is unlike anyone else who has ever been, or will ever be, born. Jesus' birth is heralded by a host of wise men who journey hundreds of miles to bow at his crib. His ministry is preceded by John the Baptist's proclamation that the Savior King of the nations and the righteous Judge of all men has arrived. At the end of Matthew 3, heaven itself opens up, and God the Father declares, "This is my Son, whom I love."[20] The beginning of Matthew 4 portrays Jesus as the new Israel who will not succumb to sin and the new Adam who will reign victorious over Satan. After all this, when Jesus comes to these fishermen and says, "Follow me, and I will make you fishers of men,"[21] one thing is abundantly clear: Jesus is not some puny religious teacher begging for an invitation from anyone. He is the all-sovereign Lord who deserves submission from everyone.

I remember the first invitation I ever received from the White House. When I opened my inbox and the subject line of the e-mail said, "From the Office of the President of the United States," I knew this was not my average correspondence. As I read the words, "The President requests the pleasure of your company on a certain date at a certain time in a certain room of the White House," I began to wonder if this was a joke or if this was real. I did some research to find out whether it was authentic, and it was.

The invitation was for the following week, and though my schedule is usually pretty full, I dropped everything I had on that day in order to be at that appointment. I quickly booked flights to Washington, DC, and made sure that I was there in plenty of time to meet with the president. I was honored to have been invited by him, and I changed everything around to respond to his invitation.

If this was my reaction—and I'm guessing yours might be similar—to a world leader of one country, a man who is in power for four, maybe eight, years, then how much more does an invitation from the everlasting, ever-reigning God of the entire universe in the flesh alter everything in our lives? Do we realize the weight of the one who has invited us to follow him? He is worthy of more than church attendance and casual association; he is worthy of total abandonment and supreme adoration.

THE KING AT THE DOOR

Yet even the illustration of an invitation from the president fails to accurately picture the invitation of Christ. For Jesus has not invited us to journey to him; instead, he has made the journey to us. What if instead of receiving an e-mail, I had received a knock at my door, and there the president invited me to meet with him?

Cody is a member of our church who moved to Thailand to share the gospel with college students. One night, a student named Annan invited Cody to go to a movie. The two of them arrived and sat down in the theater to watch the film, but before it began, a video was shown about the king of Thailand. Immediately, everyone in the theater rose and applauded, including Annan. Some people began to cry tears of joy. As this short video played, people were visibly moved simply by the sight of their king on the screen.

When the movie ended and Cody and Annan walked out of the theater, Cody asked, "Why did everyone react with such emotion when the video about the Thai king was played?"

Annan responded, "Oh, Cody, we love, respect, and honor our king, for he is a king who cares for his people. Our king will often leave his palace and come to villages and communities in Thailand to be with the people—to know them and identify with them. We know that our king loves the Thai people, and we love him."

As Cody listened, he knew that this description was setting the stage for him to share the story of a much greater King. In the days to come, Cody told Annan about how God, the King over all the universe, loved us so much that he came to us in the person of Jesus. He came to identify with us, even to the point of taking all our sin upon himself, in order to save us and to make it possible for us to follow him. Upon understanding this glorious reality, Annan became a follower of Jesus—not because he had been pursuing King Jesus, but because he realized that King Jesus had pursued him.

MATTERS OF LOVE

Do you realize the wonder of this? Marvel at the majesty of the one who left his throne in glory to come to you and me. To multitudes of people in this world, this is the most outlandish of all claims.

"God would not debase himself by becoming a man," a group of Muslim men told me in the Middle East. We were sitting together in a restaurant during Ramadan, the Islamic holy month during which Muslims fast during the day. We were eating dinner after sundown, and they began to ask me what I believe about God. In response, I began to share about Jesus.

When I told them that God had come to us in the person of Jesus, one of the men, Raahil, stopped me and said, "That is not true. God would never do that. His character is too great."

I replied, "I agree that God's character is great, and that is precisely why he came to earth as a man."

"I don't understand," Raahil responded.

I said, "Let me tell you a story and then ask you a question." Raahil consented, and I continued. "The story is about me and a girl. I loved this girl, and I wanted to marry her. So when it came time for me to tell her how much I loved her and to ask her to marry me, do you think that I sent one of my friends to relay that message for me?"

Raahil replied, "No, of course not. You need to be the one to tell her that you love her and to ask her to marry you."

I said, "Exactly. I needed to go to her and tell her myself, because in matters of love, one must go himself, right?"

Raahil responded, "Yes, that is right."

Then I replied, "This is how God shows the greatness of his character toward us. He has not ultimately sent this person or that prophet, this message or that messenger to communicate his love for us. Instead, he has come himself, because in matters of love, one must go himself."

Raahil sat back and smiled. I couldn't help but think that for the first time his heart was opening to the idea that God displays the greatness of his love not by staying distant from us, but by coming directly to us.

THE BIBLE'S CLIMACTIC QUESTION

Indeed, Jesus has come to us, as a human like us, in order to provide for us. He came to live the life we could not live—a life of total and perfect obedience to God. He never once sinned, a fact that uniquely enables him to be our Savior. Supposed Christians who deny the sinlessness of Christ demonstrate that they do not truly know Jesus, for he is only able to save because he had no sin.

Jesus came to live the life we could not live and to die the death that we deserve to die. We have already seen that even one sin before an infinitely holy and eternal God warrants infinite and eternal punishment. And this is why Jesus came: to endure the holy wrath of God due us.

My book *Radical* attracted publicity in a variety of different places. In one particular news article, a *Birmingham News* reporter made the following comment about the book: "While it's a common pulpit truism that 'God hates sin but loves the sinner,' Platt argues that God hates sinners."[22] Indeed, it was a direct quote from the book, but the article included no context from which the quote was taken. Concerned church members started asking me, "Pastor, do you believe that God hates sinners?" People in the city e-mailed me, not so kindly, saying, "You're preaching hatred in that church and all over our city."

This is one of those places where I found myself in a bit of trouble for quoting the Bible. Does God hate sinners? Listen closely to Psalm 5:5-6: "The arrogant cannot stand in your presence; you hate all who do wrong. You destroy those who tell lies; bloodthirsty and deceitful men the LORD abhors."

Wow. Maybe I shouldn't have said God hates sinners. Maybe I should have said that he abhors and destroys them.

This is not an isolated statement in Scripture. Fourteen times in the first fifty psalms alone we read of God's hatred toward the sinner, his wrath toward the liar, and so on. And the Old Testament doesn't stand alone on this. In John 3—that chapter where we have one of the most famous verses about God's love (John 3:16)—we also have one of the most neglected verses about God's wrath (John 3:36): "Whoever rejects the Son will not see life, for God's wrath remains on him."

So all of this raises the question, Is it really true that God hates the sin but loves the sinner? Well, yes, of course, in one sense, but not completely.

Think about it. As we have already seen all the way back in

Genesis, our sin is not something that exists outside of us. Sin is ingrained into the core of our being. We don't just sin; we exist as sinners. So when Jesus went to the cross to die, he was not just taking the payment of sin, as if it were separate from us. He was not just dying for our lusting or our lying or our cheating or our other sins. Instead, he was paying the price that was due us as sinners. He was dying for us, in our place, as our substitute. In the words of Isaiah 53, "He was pierced for *our* transgressions, he was crushed for *our* iniquities . . . and the LORD has laid on him the iniquity of *us* all."[23] When Jesus was pulverized under the weight of God's wrath on the cross, he was experiencing what you and I deserve to experience. He was enduring the full punishment due you and me as sinners.

Therefore, we must be careful not to lean on comfortable clichés that rob the cross of its meaning. The startling reality of Scripture is clear: we are sinners. In the words of Isaiah, "We all, like sheep, have gone astray."[24] Meanwhile, God is holy, possessing righteous wrath toward sin and sinners alike. Yet God is also merciful, possessing holy love toward sinners. So how can God show both righteous wrath and holy love toward sinners at the same time?

This is the climactic question of the Bible, and the answer is the cross of Christ. At the cross of Christ, God shows the full expression of both his wrath and his love, as Jesus is stricken, smitten, afflicted, wounded, crushed, and chastised for the sake of sinners.

Does God hate sinners? Absolutely. Look at the cross. Jesus is enduring what we are due.

Does God love sinners? Absolutely. Look at the cross. Jesus is saving us from all we are due.

Sometimes I ask people, "How do you know you are a Christian?" Or "How do you know you are saved from your sin?" The most common replies I hear from professing Christians are "Because I decided to trust in Jesus" or "Because I asked Jesus to save me however many years ago" or even "Because I have given my life to Jesus." Notice how each of these replies begins with the words, "Because I . . ." Such responses are not wrong, and I assure you my aim is not to be the word police, but I do want to offer what I hope is a healthy reminder that you and I are not saved from our sin primarily because *we* decided to do something however many years ago. Instead, we are saved from our sin ultimately because *Jesus* decided to do something two thousand years ago. And based upon his grace, his mercy, and his love in coming to us, sinners totally unable to save ourselves, we have been invited to follow him. The love of God in the life and death of Christ is the *only* foundation for authentic salvation.

THE SEEKING GOD

Earlier I described how Heather and I were planning to adopt our son Caleb before he was even born, just as God had planned to adopt his children before they were ever born. This is what Paul means when he says that

The God and Father of our Lord Jesus Christ . . . chose
us in him before the creation of the world to be holy and
blameless in his sight. In love he predestined us to be

adopted as his sons through Jesus Christ, in accordance with his pleasure and will—to the praise of his glorious grace, which he has freely given us in the One he loves.[25]

These words evoke awe and amazement, don't they? To consider that before the sun was ever formed, before a star was ever placed in the sky, before mountains were ever laid upon the earth, and before oceans were ever poured over the land, God Almighty on high set his sights on the Christian's soul. Such truth is mind-boggling and breathtaking at the same time.

Not only did he plan to love his children, but he also pursues us with his love. Over and above our sinful rebellion and selfish resistance, God in Christ pursues his people. Like a shepherd who leaves ninety-nine sheep in order to find one that is lost, God seeks after his people.[26]

This image took on entirely new meaning for me one day when I was with a group of Bedouin families in a North African desert, most of whom had never even heard about Jesus. My friend Mark knew the head of a household in a particular Bedouin tribe. The man's name was Zayed, and he had invited Mark and me to visit him when his tribe was near a particular road. So we drove for many miles into what seemed like the middle of nowhere until we came upon these nomadic people.

As soon as we stepped out of the car, I felt like I had been transported back in time. We walked into the desert and met men and women sitting under large tents that provided shade from the scorching sun overhead. We were surrounded by livestock of various kinds, and Zayed invited us to sit down with him and the others right next to a herd of sheep and goats. In gracious hospitality, they served us snacks and began boiling a milk-like drink over a makeshift stove they had assembled in the ground.

As we sat with them, we talked about where they had been traveling recently and how they had been living off the land. Bedouin herdsmen lead their families through the desert from place to place, setting up shelter and finding food and water in different settings according to different seasons. Their animals are their livelihood, and tending them daily is their occupation.

So as we talked, I told them the story of the lost sheep in Luke 15. I told them how Jesus had described a shepherd who lost one sheep out of a hundred, yet he left the ninety-nine behind in order to go in search of that one. When he found it, he hoisted it up on his shoulders and brought it back, where everyone celebrated the sheep that had been found.

As I finished telling the story, everyone around me was nodding their heads. Zayed said to me, "Every one of our sheep is valuable. If I were to lose just one of them, I would go absolutely crazy trying to find it. I would not be able to sleep until I found it. And when I found it, I would be so happy, and my family would rejoice with me."

I smiled and then said to Zayed, his family, and his friends, "This story is a picture of God's love for us. God has created us, and we are valuable to him. And even though we have wandered away from him, he comes searching after us. In what seems absolutely crazy to most people, God sent his Son to die on the cross for our sin so that we could be saved by him." I continued, "Just as you go to great lengths searching after your sheep, I want you to know that God goes to great lengths searching after his children until they are found by him."

THE OVERCOMING GRACE OF GOD

But surely the searching love of God must be believed, someone might say. God is not the only one working in salvation, is he? A man or woman must choose to receive or reject the mercy of God in Christ, right?

Absolutely. The mystery of God's mercy in no way negates the nature of man's responsibility. This entire book revolves around the decision each one of us makes to follow Jesus. But lest we ever think that such a decision begins with an invitation born out of our own initiative, the Bible clearly reminds us that left to ourselves, we would be lost forever. The only reason we can seek Christ in our sinfulness is because Christ has sought us as our Savior. The glory of the gospel is that the God of the universe reaches beyond the hardness of our hearts, overcoming our selfish resistance and sinful rebellion, and he saves us from ourselves. Such mercy magnifies God's pursuit of us and crucifies our pride before him.

When Heather and I arrived in Kazakhstan to adopt Caleb, we were met at the airport by a young woman named Vitalina. She was our translator for the next four weeks, going everywhere with us during our time in Caleb's city. After we met her, she directed Heather and me to a taxi, where we all took our seats for the ride to the orphanage.

"What kind of work do you do?" Vitalina asked me.

"I'm a pastor," I said.

She responded bluntly, "A pastor? Why are you a pastor? Don't you know that there is no such thing as God? God is for the weak."

I smiled and replied, "That's true. I am weak, and God is strong. He has done something for me and in me that I could never have done myself."

This was the beginning of daily conversations with Vitalina about who God is and how God loves. Every opportunity we had, Heather and I shared about how God had loved us enough to adopt us as his children through Christ, and how that love was now the motivation behind our desire to adopt Caleb. Over that four-week span, Vitalina listened to us constantly talk about the faithful pursuit of a God who comes to us in our weakness and captivates us with his love.

Then it happened. It was our last night in Caleb's city, and we were preparing to board our plane. After we had received our tickets and loaded our luggage, Vitalina pulled me aside. "I need to tell you something," she said.

"Okay," I replied, "what is it?"

"Last night, I realized that God does exist, and I recognized that he had sent you all here in his pursuit of me." She continued, "He has done something for me and in me that I never could have imagined. Last night, I repented of my sin and became a follower of Jesus." Then she said with excitement, "Now I am a child of God!"

As joy leaped inside my heart, a smile spread across my face. I celebrated with Vitalina, encouraged her, and prayed for her. Time was short, though, and the plane was ready to leave. So I picked up Caleb, and as Heather and I boarded the plane, we looked back, holding a child in our arms while waving good-bye to a child in God's arms.

I praise God that he has not left the invitation to salvation up to sinful men and women who in their rebellion would never choose him. I praise God that he has taken the initiative to call and enable us to follow Jesus, so that in his overcoming grace we might find eternal satisfaction for our souls.

To be a Christian is to be loved by God, pursued by God, and found by God. To be a Christian is to realize that in your sin, you were separated from God's presence, and you deserved nothing but God's wrath. Yet despite your darkness and in your deadness, his light shone on you and his voice spoke to you, inviting you to follow him. His majesty captivated your soul and his mercy covered your sin, and by his death he brought you life. Do you know for sure that you are his child, not ultimately because of any good you have done—any prayers you have prayed, steps you have taken, or boxes you have checked—but solely because of the grace he has given?

CHAPTER 3

SUPERFICIAL RELIGION AND SUPERNATURAL REGENERATION

CHRISTIANITY IS RADICALLY DIFFERENT from every other religion in the world. I saw this illustrated clearly during a recent trip to India, where I found myself working in distinctly Hindu, Muslim, Buddhist, and Sikh communities on different days.

One day I was at the Ganges River. Hindus consider the Ganges to be a holy body of water, and every year millions travel to this river to bathe in it, stand beside its waters, or perform ceremonial rites over it. According to Vedic traditions (the virtual basis for Hindu belief and practice), Hindus believe that the Ganges is a source of spiritual purification, so they wash themselves in the river in order to cleanse their sins. They also believe that the Ganges is a passageway from death to life, so they cremate deceased loved ones at the base of the Ganges and then scatter their ashes in the river, ensuring instant salvation (some don't even cremate the body of their loved one, but simply cast the body into the river). When men and women leave the Ganges, they take small amounts of water with them for use in rituals back in the villages or towns where they live. Hinduism prescribes a variety of different rituals to a variety of different gods, and Hindus believe that the path to remission of sins and liberation from the cycle of life and death is paved through homage to the Ganges (or more specifically, the goddess Ganga that is represented by the river).

On another day, in another part of the region, I heard calls to prayer resounding from loudspeakers at five separate times during the day. Muslims responded by filing into mosques and completing a series of prayers that involved bowing down with their hands on their knees, prostrating their faces to the ground, and then rising to stand. According to the words of Muhammad in the Koran, these times of prayer are required for Muslims to honor Allah, each occurring at prescribed times with prescribed procedures under prescribed conditions.

Yet another day, we visited a training center for Tibetan Buddhists. Over five hundred Buddhist monks live on this property, complete with a monastery, library, training school, and two large temples. Everywhere we looked, we saw worshipers bowing before statues of gold and stone. People walked in circles, reciting mantras and spinning prayer wheels. Following the teachings of the Buddha, these monks believe in following an eightfold path that consists of right views, right aspiration, right speech, right conduct, right livelihood, right effort, right mindfulness, and right contemplation. If a monk is willing to follow this slow, difficult road to salvation, he believes he will experience eventual nirvana, which includes freedom from all desire and suffering.

I asked one of the monks why he did what he did. He responded, "Because I want to find peace and rest."

I asked, "How will you find peace and rest?"

He answered, "I don't know; I'm still searching."

During our final evening in India, we spent time in a Sikh community, where people were assembling to honor the traditional teaching of the ten gurus who together established and defined Sikhism. Forbidden to cut their hair, men wore turbans of different colors and women covered their heads. They entered the temple and bowed before the Sikh scriptures, known as the Guru Granth Sahib. This holy book describes the way to truth and life, and it is the center of Sikh worship. After bowing before the book, men and women then received a free meal in a small bowl, for sharing with others is a traditional sign of the Sikh religion.

Looking back on these four encounters with four major religions in the world, I realized that they all shared one common denominator: in every religion, a teacher (or a series of teachers) prescribes certain paths to follow in order to honor God (or different gods) and experience salvation (however that is described).

In Hinduism, ancient teachers have passed down Vedic traditions prescribing rites and rituals for Hindus to observe. In Islam, Muhammad pointed in the Koran to five pillars for Muslims to practice. In Buddhism, the Buddha's eightfold path is just one of four noble truths that he taught, alongside hundreds of other rules for Buddhists to follow. In Sikhism, ten gurus have pointed to one body of teaching as the way to truth and life.

But this is where Christianity stands alone. When Jesus came on the scene in human history and began calling followers to himself, he did not say, "Follow certain rules. Observe specific regulations. Perform ritual duties. Pursue a particular path." Instead, he said, "Follow *me*."

With these two simple words, Jesus made clear that his primary purpose was not to instruct his disciples in a prescribed religion; his primary purpose was to invite his disciples into a personal relationship. He was not saying, "Go this way to find truth and life." Instead, he was saying, "*I am* the way and the truth and the life."[1] The call of Jesus was, "Come to *me*. Find rest for your souls in *me*. Find joy in your heart from *me*. Find meaning in your life through *me*."

This extremely shocking and utterly revolutionary call is the essence of what it means to be a disciple of Jesus: we are not called to simply believe certain points or observe certain practices, but ultimately to cling to the person of Christ as life itself.

But we have missed this. In so many ways and in so many settings, we have relegated Christianity to just another choice in the cafeteria line of world religions. Slowly and subtly, we have let Christianity devolve into just another set of rules, regulations, practices, and principles to observe. Hindus bathe in the Ganges River; Christians get baptized in the church. Muslims go to worship on Friday; Christians go to worship on Sunday. Buddhists recite mantras; Christians sing choruses. Sikhs read their holy book and share with the needy; Christians read their Bibles and give to the poor. Now don't get me wrong: I am definitely not saying that we should not be baptized, sing in worship, read our Bibles, or serve the poor. But I am saying that if we are not careful, any one of us can do all of these things completely apart from Jesus.

THE BURDEN OF RULES

Think about whom Jesus was speaking to when he said, "Follow me." These Galilean fishermen were surrounded by a religious establishment that was consumed with rules and regulations. Teachers of the law had taken the commands of God in the Old Testament and twisted them to become the principal means by which one could earn God's favor. Additionally, they had tacked on miscellaneous other instructions that people were expected to follow as devout Jewish men and women.

For example, God's law in the Old Testament commanded God's people not to travel on the Sabbath. Invariably, teachers of the law began to ask, "Well, what constitutes traveling? Can you travel around your house? Can you travel to someone else's house? If you travel beyond someone else's house, how far can you go?" In response, these teachers laid down a new law, saying, "You can travel three thousand feet from your house on the Sabbath. One exception to this is if you have food that is within three thousand feet of your house to eat on the Sabbath. If that's the case, then that food is an extension of your house, and you can travel three thousand feet from the place where your food is." Basically, if you put food in the right places, you could spend the Sabbath traveling all over town.

Similarly, the law said that you could not carry a load on the Sabbath. But the teachers asked, "What is considered a load? Are your clothes a load?" In turn, these teachers said that as long as you are wearing your clothes, they are not a load. But if you are carrying an item of clothing, it is considered a load. So it would be okay to *wear* a jacket on the Sabbath, but it would be wrong to *carry* a jacket on the Sabbath. One writer says,

> Tailors did not carry a needle with them on the Sabbath for fear they might be tempted to mend a garment and thereby perform work. Nothing could be bought or sold, and clothing could not be dyed or washed. . . . Chairs could not be moved because dragging them might make a furrow in the ground, and a woman was not to look in a mirror lest she see a gray hair and be tempted to pull it out.[2]

In addition to such Sabbath regulations, all sorts of other rules dominated the day in which the disciples lived.

This background makes the words of Jesus all the more refreshing. "Come to me," he said in Matthew 11, "all you who are weary and burdened, and I will give you rest. Take my yoke upon you and learn from me, for I am gentle and humble in heart, and you will find rest for your souls."[3] These words from Jesus tenderly resound in a world where every other religious teacher says, "Try harder, work harder, do more, and become better."

Clearly our greatest need is not more regulations in order to merit salvation. We have already seen that our lives are filled with sin and we cannot save ourselves. No matter how many times we wash our bodies in a river or pray according to procedure, regardless of how many steps we take down a path or how many needy people we help, and despite our most passionate attempts to pray the right prayers, repeat the right words, sing the right songs, give the right gifts, and live the right lives, we cannot cover up the evil that is entrenched so deeply within our hearts. Our greatest need is not to try harder. Our greatest need is a new heart.

SPINNING PLATES FOR GOD

Jesus did not come so that we might live a life of superficial religion. He came so that we might receive new life through supernatural regeneration. Let me explain the difference.

Superficial religion consists of merely believing certain truths and doing certain things. As we've already seen in discussing different faiths, such superficial religion is rampant in the world today, and it was rampant in the world of Jesus' day as well. Think about his conversation with Nicodemus, a leader among the Jewish people in the first century. Nicodemus was like many professing Christians today, possessing a measure of belief in and respect for Jesus while ordering his life around the commands of Scripture. He prayed and went to worship. He read and even taught the Bible. He lived a good, decent, moral life, and he was an example to others. Moreover, he did all of this in an effort to honor God. Everything was right on the outside, but something was wrong on the inside. Despite all the religious things he did, Nicodemus had no spiritual life in him.

Do you ever feel like that? Do you ever feel like your Christianity consists of nothing more than a list of truths to believe, things to do, and boxes to check in order to earn God's approval? In your efforts to pray, read the Bible, give, and serve in the church, do you ever feel like you're never doing enough? Like the plate spinner who entertains audiences by trying to keep all kinds of plates in the air at the same time, do you ever tire of trying to please God with your performance? In the end, do you feel like your faith is mainly duty with minimal delight?

This is the curse of superficial religion: the constant attempt to do outward things apart from inward transformation. One writer describes the Christian version of superficial religion this way:

> You . . . seek to be godly by submitting yourself to external rules and regulations and by conforming to behavior patterns imposed upon you by the particular Christian society that you have chosen and in which you hope to be found "acceptable." You will in this way perpetuate the pagan habit of practicing religion in the energy of the flesh, and in the very pursuit of righteousness commit idolatry in honoring "Christianity" more than Christ![4]
>
> In defiance of God's Word, God's mind, God's will, and God's judgment, men [and women] everywhere are prepared to dedicate to God what God condemns—the energy of the flesh! There is nothing quite so nauseating or pathetic as the flesh trying to be holy![5]

A NEW HEART

So how did Jesus respond to the superficial religion of Nicodemus? He told him, "No one can see the kingdom of God unless he is born again." Then he elaborated on this a couple of verses later, saying, "No one can enter the kingdom of God unless he is born of water and the Spirit."[6] So what does that mean?

Jesus references a promise here that God had made to his people through the prophet Ezekiel hundreds of years before his conversation with Nicodemus. Back in Ezekiel 36, God told his people,

I will sprinkle clean water on you, and you will be clean;
I will cleanse you from all your impurities and from all
your idols. I will give you a new heart and put a new spirit
in you; I will remove from you your heart of stone and
give you a heart of flesh. And I will put my Spirit in you
and move you to follow my decrees and be careful to keep
my laws. You will live in the land I gave your forefathers;
you will be my people, and I will be your God.[7]

Do you see the link between being born of water and the Spirit? Jesus is pointing out God's promise to give his people a new heart. This new heart would first and foremost be cleansed of sin, "[cleansed] from all your impurities." God spoke similarly through the prophet Jeremiah, promising his people, "I will put my law in their minds and write it on their hearts. . . . I will forgive their wickedness and will remember their sins no more."[8]

This is exactly what Jesus came to do. The New Testament announces his coming, saying that "he will save his people from their sins."[9] When John the Baptist first sees Jesus, John shouts, "Look, the Lamb of God, who takes away the sin of the world!"[10]

Imagery of God washing away his people's sin fills Scripture.

"Though your sins are like scarlet," God says, "they shall be as white as snow."[11] David prays, "Wash away all my iniquity and cleanse me from my sin."[12] These Old Testament pictures provide a foretaste of the forgiveness that ultimately comes through Christ in the New Testament. Speaking to people who used to be characterized by sin-saturated lives, Paul says, "You were washed, you were sanctified, you were justified in the name of the Lord Jesus Christ."[13] John writes, "If we confess our sins, he is faithful and just to forgive us our sins and to cleanse us from all unrighteousness."[14]

Such cleansing is a gift from God not based at all upon our merit, but altogether upon God's mercy. In the words of Paul, "When the kindness and love of God our Savior appeared, he saved us, not because of righteous things we had done, but because of his mercy. He saved us through the washing of rebirth."[15] The clear message of the Bible is that there is nothing we can do to make our hearts clean before a holy God. We can work constantly, pray fervently, give extravagantly, and love sacrificially, but our hearts will still be stained by sin.

This is why the Bible teaches that faith alone in Christ alone is the only way to salvation from sin. Faith is the *anti*-work. It's the realization that there is nothing you can do but trust in what has been done for you in the life, death, and resurrection of Jesus. Faith is the realization that God's pleasure in you will never be based upon your performance for him. Instead, God's pleasure in you will always be based upon Christ's performance for you.

From every Hindu at the Ganges River to every reader of this book, the invitation is clear: come to Christ, and he will cleanse your heart. Hear the revolutionary truth of the gospel: we do not have to work to wash away our sins. As we turn from our sin to trust in Christ, we receive a new, clean heart, and God in his grace remembers our sins no more.

NO RECORD

I heard a story once about an Englishman who bought a Rolls-Royce. It had been advertised as the car that would never, ever, ever break down. So the man bought the Rolls-Royce at a hefty price and was driving it one day when, to his surprise, it broke down. He was far away from town, so he called Rolls-Royce and said, "Hey, you know this car that will never break down? Well, it's broken down."

Immediately, a Rolls-Royce mechanic was sent via helicopter to the location where the car was broken down. The car was fixed, and the man went on his way. Naturally, the man expected to get a bill from Rolls-Royce. It was clearly expensive for them to provide such service (not often does a mechanic fly to where your car is broken down!), and he wanted to get the whole ordeal behind him. So when the bill had not yet come a few weeks later, the man called Rolls-Royce and said, "I'd like to go ahead and pay the bill for my auto repairs so that we can get this behind us." Rolls-Royce responded, "Sir, we are deeply sorry, but we have absolutely no record of anything ever having gone wrong with your car."

Consider the wonder. For all who come to Christ and receive a new heart from him, the God of the universe looks at you and says, "I have absolutely no record of anything ever having gone wrong in your life."

OUR GREATEST NEED

This is the Good News of the Kingdom, and it meets the greatest need in our lives. Through Jesus, God forgives our sins and reconciles us to himself. Yet if we're not careful, we will subtly skew this Good News and ultimately ignore our greatest need.

All around the world today, people are equating the gospel of Jesus Christ with physical healing and material prosperity. "Come to Jesus," they say, "and you will receive physical reward." But that is not the essence of the gospel. Yes, Jesus is able to heal physical maladies, and yes, Jesus has authority over painful diseases, but this is not the central message of Christ. We don't go throughout America, saying, "Trust in Christ, and cancer will be gone." We don't go throughout Africa, declaring, "Trust in Christ, and HIV/ AIDS will be no more." We don't go anywhere, crying, "Trust in Christ, and health and wealth will come your way."

That is not the Good News of Christ, for the Good News of Christ is so much greater than that. The Good News of Christ is not primarily that Jesus will heal you of all your sicknesses right now, but ultimately that Jesus will forgive you of all your sins forever. The Good News of Christ is not that if you muster enough faith in Jesus, you can have physical and material reward on this earth. The Good News of Christ is that when you have childlike faith in Jesus, you will be reconciled to God for eternity.

We mustn't be like the paralyzed man and his friends in Matthew 9, approaching Jesus as a miracle worker who was merely able to meet immediate physical needs. To their surprise, though they expected Jesus to heal the man physically, Jesus' first response was "Take heart, son; your sins are forgiven."[16] In these words he made clear that the ultimate priority of his coming was not simply to relieve suffering but to sever the root of suffering: sin. And this is our greatest need.

For years, my mother-in-law struggled with diabetes, breast cancer, neuropathy, degenerative eye disease, hand surgeries, and foot pain. Through it all, she would have said that she was a Christian. She believed in Jesus and lived a decent, kind, good, generous life. Yet she was just like Nicodemus. Though she knew truth about Jesus, she needed to be born again.

Then one day, everything changed. For the first time, my mother-in-law realized the depth of her need for God's grace in Christ, she turned from herself and her sin, and she trusted in Jesus as the Lord over her life. God, in his mercy, gave her a new heart, cleansed of sin and confident in him.

Yet at the same time she experienced evident spiritual regeneration, she experienced deeper physical degeneration. Her kidneys began to fail, and she was admitted to the hospital on various occasions. Then one night, all of a sudden, she experienced an unexpected brain hemorrhage and died.

So what happened? Did Jesus fail her at her greatest time of need? Absolutely not. In reality, Jesus had healed her at her deepest point of need, and she knew that she could trust in him. The testimony of her life—and her death—is clear: you can trust Christ when you have diabetes, you can trust him when you get diagnosed with breast cancer, you can trust him with your neuropathy, you can trust him with degenerative eye disease, you can trust him when you have kidney failure, and you can trust him when massive bleeding takes over your brain because in the middle of it all, you know that Jesus has met the deepest need of your heart. You know that you have been cleansed of all your sin and have nothing to fear before him. And you know that when this body can't take it any longer, you breathe your last breath, and your heart stops beating, you have no reason to worry because you have united your life with the man who conquered death, the only one who severed sin as the root of all suffering, and so you say with Scripture, "Where, O death, is your victory? Where, O death, is your sting? The sting of death is sin, and the power of sin is the law. But thanks be to God! He gives us the victory through our Lord Jesus Christ."[17]

Forgiveness is God's greatest gift because it meets our greatest need. More than we need to be healed of cancer, we need to be cleansed of sin. More than we need a tumor removed, we need our sins forgotten. And this is exactly what Jesus gives us in a new heart, cleansed of sin, that leaves us with nothing to fear now and forever.

A NEW SPIRIT

Yet this is not where Christianity stops. So often we put a period on this point and assume that the essence of the Christian life is being forgiven of our sin. Many professing Christians are stuck here, believing that Jesus has cleansed them from their sins, yet lacking true, authentic, real, radical change in their lives.

But this is not the way it's supposed to be, for there is more to God's promise in Ezekiel. God told his people, "I will give you a new heart and put a new *spirit* in you. . . . I will put my *Spirit* in you and move you to follow my decrees and be careful to keep my laws."[18]

In light of this, Jesus told Nicodemus that to be born again means to be born of water and of *Spirit*. The meaning behind these words is mind-blowing. When you come to Jesus, he not only forgives you of your sin, but he also fills you with his Spirit. Christian, feel the magnitude of this: when you come to Jesus, he puts the source of his life in the center of your life.

This is the heart of Jesus' call to follow him. When you become a Christian, you die, and Jesus becomes your life. To paraphrase Paul, "You have died with Christ, and you're not even alive anymore. Instead, Christ is alive in you, and the only way you live is by faith in him."[19] Paul later writes, "If Christ is in you, your body is dead because of sin, yet your spirit is alive because of righteousness. And if the Spirit of him who raised Jesus from the dead is living in you, he who raised Christ from the dead will also give life to your mortal bodies through his Spirit, who lives in you."[20] This is the stunning message of Christianity: Jesus died for you so that he might live in you. Jesus doesn't merely improve your old nature; he imparts to you an entirely new nature—one that is completely united with his.

When Heather and I were engaged in the year before we were married, we were living totally different lives. I was finishing college and living on little income (i.e., I had no cash flow). I was eating ramen noodles for most of my meals and struggling to get by. Meanwhile, Heather had graduated from college and was teaching in an elementary school. This meant that she had an income (i.e., she had cash flow), and she didn't have to eat ramen noodles.

After twelve months of waiting to be married, we finally stood in front of a crowd of our friends and family, ready to commit our lives to each other. On that wedding day, I received so many wonderful things, the most important of which was a beautiful, godly wife. But do you know what else I received on that day?

Cash flow.

It was great. At one moment, I had nothing in my bank account. But the moment I said, "I do," I had everything that was in her bank account. And I didn't have to do anything to earn it. I didn't have to go to her school and teach her five-year-olds. I didn't have to get a job anywhere else, for that matter. Simply because my life was now united with Heather's, everything that belonged to her became mine.

In a much, much greater way, when you come to Jesus—when you unite your life with his—everything that belongs to him becomes yours. Yes, as we've already discussed, his righteousness replaces your unrighteousness. But there's more. When you come to Jesus, his Spirit fills your spirit. His love becomes your love. His joy becomes your joy. His mind becomes your mind. His desires become your desires. His will becomes your will. His purpose becomes your purpose. His power becomes your power. The Christian life thus becomes nothing less than the outliving of the indwelling Christ.

This reality marks the critical distinction between superficial religion and supernatural regeneration. Superficial religion involves a counterfeit "Christian" life that consists of nothing more than truths to believe and things to do, and it misses the essence of what it means to follow Jesus. Supernatural regeneration, on the other hand, involves an authentic Christian life that has been awakened by the Spirit, truth, love, passion, power, and purpose of Jesus.

FROM BEING DISCIPLES TO MAKING DISCIPLES

This is exactly what Jesus means in the words that he says right after "Follow me." If you'll remember, he told those four fishermen, "Follow me, and *I will make you* fishers of men."[21] Notice in his invitation that Jesus does not tell his disciples what he will *call* them to do. Instead, Jesus tells them what he will *cause* them to do. The commands he would give *to* them could only be accomplished by the work that he would do *in* them. As these disciples followed Jesus, he would transform everything about their lives: their thoughts, their desires, their wills, their relationships, and ultimately the very purpose for which they lived.

And this is where things got really interesting. "Follow me," Jesus said, "and I will make you *fishers of men*." Using imagery familiar to these disciples' long-standing vocation, Jesus summoned them to an all-consuming mission right from the start. More important than searching for fish all over the sea, they would spread the gospel all over the world. As a result of being disciples of Jesus, they would make disciples of Jesus. For every one of these disciples, following Jesus would lead to fishing for men. Not surprisingly, the book of Matthew ends with Jesus on a mountainside, saying to these same disciples, "Go and make disciples of all nations, baptizing them in the name of the Father and of the Son and of the Holy Spirit, and teaching them to obey everything I have commanded you. And surely I am with you always, to the very end of the age."[22]

Somewhere between Matthew 4 and Matthew 28, Jesus had caused these disciples to become disciple makers. He had transformed these followers into fishermen, and by the time they got to that mountain in Matthew 28, they were eager to tell everyone about the life, death, and resurrection of Jesus. Having been forgiven of their sin and soon to be filled with God's Spirit, they would give their lives not simply to *being* disciples of Jesus, but sacrificially to *making* disciples of Jesus. Fishing for men would become central for them—and costly to them.

Peter preached the gospel to thousands at Pentecost and to throngs thereafter, and because he would not shut up, as we've already seen, tradition says he was crucified upside down. Similar traditions tell us that Andrew was crucified while preaching the gospel in Greece, Judas (not Iscariot) was clubbed to death for ministering near modern-day Turkey, Thomas was speared through his side while making disciples in India, James was beheaded, Philip was stoned, and Matthew was burned at the stake, all for preaching the gospel. As a result of being disciples of Jesus, every one of these men literally gave their lives to making disciples of Jesus.

Clearly, the overflow of transformation *in* these disciples was multiplication *through* these disciples. As Jesus transformed their minds, they became convicted that people needed to hear the gospel. As Jesus transformed their desires, they longed for people to hear the gospel. As Jesus transformed their wills, they were compelled to give their lives proclaiming the gospel. As Jesus transformed their relationships, they loved people enough to share the gospel with them, even though it cost them everything they had. Jesus had transformed their very purpose for living—every disciple was sacrificially committed to making disciples—and the trajectory of their lives was never the same.

All of this makes me wonder what we're missing. When I look

at the church today, it seems like we have taken the costly command of Christ to go, baptize, and teach all nations and mutated it into a comfortable call for Christians to come, be baptized, and sit in one location. If you ask individual Christians today what it practically means to make disciples, you will likely get jumbled thoughts, ambiguous answers, and probably even some blank stares. We seem to have exempted one another from any personal responsibility to fish for men, and I'm convinced that the majority of professing Christians would not say their purpose in this life is to make disciples of all nations. In fact, most would shrink back from this thought, and some readers may even be tempted to close the book at this point for bringing up the very idea. *This is no longer for me*, you might think.

But please don't close the book. Think about it with me. Biblically, isn't every single disciple of Jesus intended to make disciples of Jesus? From the very beginning of Christianity, hasn't following Jesus always involved fishing for men? And doesn't it seem like these early disciples of Jesus made disciples of Jesus not because they had to, but because they wanted to? Those first disciples on the mountain in Matthew 28 did not have to be superficially cajoled into making disciples; they were supernaturally compelled to do it. Not even death could stop them from obeying this command.

So what is keeping us from obeying this command today? I mean every single one of us. Why are so many supposed Christians sitting on the sidelines of the church, maybe even involved in the machinery of the church, but not wholeheartedly, passionately, sacrificially, and joyfully giving their lives to making disciples of all the nations? Could it be because so many people in the church have settled for superficial religion instead of supernatural regeneration?

SUPERNATURAL OVERFLOW

If Christianity merely consists of a list of dutiful dos and don'ts on top of principles to believe and practices to observe—many of which are similar to every other religion—then we don't have much to share with the world. Why become a Christian when Islam or Hinduism feels fundamentally the same? Aren't all people simply following rules that fit with their religious customs, and in the end won't all people be rewarded for that in some way?

Further, if being a Christian is merely a matter of superficial religion, then no amount of persuasion will convince us that we need to step out of our comfort zones, alter our priorities, sacrifice our possessions, risk our reputations, and potentially even lose our lives to share Christ with others. We have every reason to sit back in a privatized faith that works well and doesn't impose upon the people around us (much less around the world). A superficial approach to Christianity always results in a spectator mentality in the church.

However, if Christianity involves supernatural regeneration whereby the God of the universe reaches down his hand of mercy into the depths of our souls, forgives us of all our sin, *and* fills us with his Spirit, then a spectator mentality is spiritually inconceivable. For people whose hearts, minds, wills, and relationships have been radically turned upside down by the person of Christ, the purpose of Christ will reign supreme.

If you are truly a disciple of Jesus, you will be supernaturally compelled to make disciples of Jesus. True followers of Jesus do not need to be convinced, cajoled, persuaded, or manipulated into making disciples of all nations. Everyone who follows Jesus biblically will fish for men globally.

I think about Tom and Jordan, whom I mentioned in the first chapter. Both were engrossed in superficial religion until Christ took hold of their hearts and transformed their lives. Immediately after he was born again, Tom began leveraging his life to lead others to Christ. He started Bible studies at his workplace. He and his wife began investing their lives into other couples in order to help them grow in Christ. In the years since his salvation, he has spread the gospel in Birmingham, South America, Eastern Europe, and the Middle East.

Likewise, upon her salvation, Jordan committed her life to making disciples on her college campus. Then she spent a couple of months in West Africa, sharing the gospel in a town of ninety thousand people, 99.8 percent of whom were Muslim. After graduation, she got married and moved with her husband into a higher-crime, lower-income area of the inner city to proclaim and live out the gospel there.

I think about Abid, a doctor who lives on the most unevangelized island on earth. Abid came from a very wealthy, extremely devout Muslim family. He had made a holy pilgrimage to Mecca seven different times. But by God's grace, through Abid's medical practice, he met Christian missionaries who shared the gospel with him. As he heard about Christ, Abid experienced a peace that had evaded him his entire life in Islam. Knowing that the cost would be steep, he became a follower of Jesus. As soon as this became known in his family, Abid was tied up and beaten. His wife left him, his kids abandoned him, he lost his medical practice, and today he lives under a constant threat of death from his extended family.

But nothing can stop Abid from making disciples. Upon his salvation, Abid had asked God to use him to share the gospel with one thousand people during his first year as a Christian. At the end of that first year, God had given him opportunity to share the Good News of God's grace in Christ with over four thousand people.

Or I think about Sanja in India, an impoverished mother of two little girls. When she became pregnant with her second daughter, her husband left her because he didn't want to have to pay the price for a man to marry his girls when they were older. In shame, Sanja was forced to live once again with her parents. Having spent her life as a Hindu woman, she was surprised to discover a church that reached out to pregnant mothers in her community. Through interaction with church members, Sanja heard about the unfailing love of God in Christ. Though it would cause her further shame in her community, she repented of her sin and trusted in Jesus. Now she helps lead the outreach from her church to other impoverished pregnant mothers, and she is sharing the gospel with every Hindu she knows.

If you were to ask Tom, Jordan, Abid, or Sanja why they make disciples, I am confident that none of them would say it's because they have to. Instead, each of them would say it's because they want to. God has given these brothers and sisters a new heart, a heart that is forgiven of sin and filled with his Spirit, and spreading the gospel is the natural—or supernatural—overflow, not of a religion they adhere to called Christianity, but of a relationship they have with Christ.

HAVE YOU BEEN BORN AGAIN?

So what about you?

Are you engulfed in superficial religion, or have you experienced supernatural regeneration? Are you concentrating on Christian principles and practices in your life, or are you clinging to Christ as your life? Are you confident that you've been forgiven of your sin, and is it clear that you are filled with his Spirit? Ultimately, have you been born again?

The fruit of following Jesus is a new heart with a new mind, new desires, a new will, a new way of relating to people around you, and a new purpose. "Follow me," Jesus said, "and I will make you fishers of men." This is not some solicitation to tread a path of superficial religion. This is an invitation to taste a pleasure that can only be found in a supernatural relationship with Jesus. He beckons you to let your heart be captivated by his greatness and your life be changed by his grace. Turn from your sin and yourself and trust in him as the all-sovereign, all-satisfying Savior of your soul.

But do not be mistaken. This does not mean that you are making Jesus your personal Lord and Savior.

CHAPTER 4

DON'T MAKE JESUS YOUR PERSONAL LORD AND SAVIOR

WHEN FOLLOWERS OF CHRIST share stories of how they became Christians, they often say something along the lines of, "I decided to make Jesus my personal Lord and Savior." Initially and ultimately, of course, it's wonderful to hear brothers and sisters recount the moment when their hearts were opened to the incomprehensibly passionate love of God—a love that now captivates them in an intimately personal relationship with Jesus. At the same time, when I reflect on that particular statement—"I decided to make Jesus my personal Lord and Savior"—I can't help but wonder how much this idea represents some subtly yet significantly dangerous trends in contemporary Christianity.

On one level, this statement minimizes the inherent authority of Jesus. Surely none of us can *decide* to make him Lord. Jesus *is* Lord regardless of what you or I decide. The Bible is clear that one day "every knee [will] bow, in heaven and on earth and under the earth, and every tongue [will] confess that Jesus Christ is Lord."[1] The question is not whether we will make Jesus Lord. The real question is whether you or I will submit to his lordship, and this is the essence of conversion.

Yet on an even deeper level, I'm afraid that we use this phrase all too often to foster a customized Christianity that revolves around a personal Christ that we create for ourselves. Almost unknowingly, we all have a tendency to redefine Christianity according to our own tastes, preferences, church traditions, and cultural norms. Slowly, subtly, we take the Jesus of the Bible and twist him into someone with whom we are a little more comfortable. We dilute what he says about the cost of following him, we disregard what he says about those who choose not to follow him, we practically ignore what he says about materialism, and we functionally miss what he says about mission. We pick and choose what we like and don't like from Jesus' teachings. In the end, we create a nice, non-offensive, politically correct, middle-class, American Jesus who looks just like us and thinks just like us.

But Jesus is not customizable. He has not left himself open to interpretation, adaptation, innovation, or alteration. He has spoken clearly through his Word, and we have no right to personalize him. Instead, he revolutionizes us. He transforms our minds through his truth. As we follow Jesus, we believe Jesus, even when his Word confronts (and often contradicts) the deeply held assumptions, beliefs, and convictions of our lives, our families, our friends, our culture, and sometimes even our churches. And as we take Jesus at his Word, we proclaim Jesus to the world, for we realize that he is not merely a personal Lord and Savior who is worthy of our individual approval. Ultimately, Jesus is the cosmic Lord and Savior who is worthy of everyone's eternal praise.

FOLLOWING REQUIRES BELIEVING

According to research, many "Christians" no longer believe that God is the supreme Creator and Ruler of the universe. Such "Christians" believe that everyone is god or that maybe god is simply the realization of one's human potential. Over half of "Christians" don't believe that the Holy Spirit or Satan is real, and tens of millions of them don't believe that Jesus is the divine Son of God. Finally, almost half of "Christians" don't believe the Bible is completely true.[2]

I put *Christians* in quotation marks for what I hope by now is an obvious reason: such "Christians" are not Christians. It is impossible to follow Jesus yet disregard, discredit, and disbelieve his Word. Simply put, to follow Jesus is to believe Jesus.

Now we've already observed how intellectual belief in Christ does not equate with saving faith in Christ. As we noted, even demons believe that Jesus died on the cross and rose from the grave.[3] Becoming and being a disciple of Jesus involves far more than mere intellectual belief in him. But it certainly doesn't involve anything less.

Believing Jesus has been fundamental to following Jesus from the beginning. When you read through the Gospels and observe Jesus' interaction with his disciples, you see him continually teaching them truth and challenging their thinking. In every story and every conversation, Jesus is turning these disciples' minds upside down with his words. Though Jesus never enrolled his disciples in a formal school or sat them down in a classroom, he used every situation, every conversation, every miracle, and every moment to mold their minds to become like his.

Then, when Jesus prepared his disciples for his death and departure, he promised them his Spirit (note: the Holy Spirit is real according to Jesus), "the Spirit of truth," who "will teach you all things and bring to your remembrance all that I have said to you."[4] To be a disciple of Jesus was (and is) to be devoted to the words of Jesus. "If you abide in my word," Jesus says, "you are truly my disciples, and you will know the truth, and the truth will set you free."[5] "If you abide in me, and my words abide in you, ask whatever you wish, and it will be done for you."[6] From the start, the promises and privileges of following Jesus with your life were tied to believing Jesus with your mind.

As the New Testament continues beyond the life of Jesus on earth, Paul talks about how disciples, through the Spirit of Christ, have the mind of Christ.[7] He urges the Roman Christians to be transformed by the renewing of their minds,[8] and he implores the Colossian Christians to "put off the old self with its practices and . . . put on the new self, which is being renewed in knowledge after the image of its creator."[9] He writes about spiritual warfare, "We demolish arguments and every pretension that sets itself up against the knowledge of God, and we take captive every thought to make it obedient to Christ."[10] According to Scripture, the minds, hearts, and lives of Christians revolve entirely around the words of Christ.

RESURRECTION AUTHORITY

But isn't it a bit crazy for you and me to base our lives in the twenty-first century on the words of a man from the first century? After all, aren't some of the Bible's teachings simply archaic? Are we really supposed to take literally everything that Jesus said? Haven't we experienced cultural developments and discovered scientific advancements since the days in which Jesus lived? How do we know that what Jesus taught two thousand years ago is still true today?

This is where we realize that the authority of Jesus' words is tied to the actuality of Jesus' resurrection. Think about it. If Jesus did not rise from the dead, then ultimately we don't have to worry about a thing he said. He would be just like every other religious teacher in the world, teaching truths and imparting opinions for how to have a better life. In fact, he would actually be far worse than other religious teachers, because he promised that he would rise from the dead and then didn't. If Jesus wasn't resurrected, then all of Christianity is a hoax and Christians are the most pitiably stupid people on the planet (the New Testament itself teaches this in 1 Corinthians 15). And if that's the case, then we are free to pick and choose whatever we want to take from Jesus that might be helpful for us.

But if Jesus *did* rise from the dead, if he did what no one else in all of history has ever done or will ever do—conquer death—then we can't just accept what Jesus said. We must orient everything in our lives around what Jesus said.

So did Jesus rise from the dead? Is he indeed Lord regardless of what you and I decide?

Some people believe that Jesus didn't even die on a cross, much less rise from the grave three days later. Many Muslims, for example, purport that it was merely a man who looked like Jesus who was crucified that day. Never mind that this theory was invented by the prophet Muhammad six centuries after the Crucifixion occurred. Others believe that though it was Jesus on the cross, he didn't actually die there. He was simply hurt really, really bad. He fainted and went unconscious, so people simply thought he was dead. This explanation assumes that Jesus went through six trials, no sleep, a brutal scourging, thorns thrust into his head, nails thrust into his hands and feet, and a spear thrust into his side after several hours on a cross. Then he fainted, was wrapped in grave clothes, and put in a tomb with a stone rolled over the entrance that was guarded by Roman soldiers. He subsequently regained consciousness, nudged the stone away from the darkness of the tomb, hopped past the guards who were standing by, and coolly went about his way. This is probably not the most plausible explanation.

Others maintain that the tomb was not empty. Some people believe what has been described as the "wrong tomb theory," that when the women went to the tomb that first Easter morning, in their grief and shock over Jesus' death, they went to the wrong tomb and mistakenly thought Jesus had risen. Ever since that day, then, everyone else has gone to the wrong tomb. If only someone would check next door. The obvious problem with this theory is that the last thing Roman (as well as Jewish) authorities wanted was a group of people claiming that their leader had risen from the dead. That's why they posted guards at the tomb in the first place. Surely they knew which tomb to guard, and even if they didn't, they could have shut down all of Christianity by simply pointing to Jesus' body in the right tomb.

Still others believe that the disciples are to blame for a concocted resurrection story. Some claim that the disciples stole the body of Jesus, which would require a small group of timid Galilean men (who the night before had been scared to admit they even knew Jesus) to outmaneuver a guard of highly skilled Roman soldiers. Others allege that the disciples were merely delusional—hallucinatory at best—when they claimed they had seen Jesus alive after he died. But even the thought of resurrection from the grave was virtually inconceivable in both Greco-Roman and Jewish thought in the first century. Nevertheless, hundreds of people claimed to have seen Jesus, some of whom ate, drank, and talked with him. Hallucinations don't normally eat and drink. Besides, it was not in the best interest of disciples for them to proclaim the resurrection of Jesus in the first century, knowing that they could (and would) die for it. In the words of Pascal, "I believe witnesses [who] got themselves killed."[11]

So why do I belabor this point? Because if Jesus actually rose from the dead, then we absolutely must listen to everything he said. The reality of his resurrection validates both the truthfulness and timelessness of his teaching. Jesus is not just another religious teacher whose thoughts and opinions we can take or leave according to our preferences. Regardless of what we might say (or decide), *Jesus is Lord*. As a result, regardless of what he might say (or declare), we have no choice but to trust his Word.

JESUS AND HELL

In light of this, consider one of the most biblically clear yet culturally controversial issues on which Jesus spoke: hell. When teaching his disciples, Jesus explained that God had given him authority to judge all people everywhere for all of eternity. Hear his words in John 5:

> The Father judges no one, but has entrusted all judgment to the Son, that all may honor the Son just as they honor the Father. He who does not honor the Son does not honor the Father, who sent him.
>
> I tell you the truth, whoever hears my word and believes him who sent me has eternal life and will not be condemned; he has crossed over from death to life. . . .
>
> For as the Father has life in himself, so he has granted the Son to have life in himself. And he has given him authority to judge because he is the Son of Man.
>
> Do not be amazed at this, for a time is coming when all who are in their graves will hear his voice and come out—those who have done good will rise to live, and those who have done evil will rise to be condemned.[12]

Later in Scripture, Revelation 20 depicts the judgment scene to which Jesus referred:

> Then I saw a great white throne and him who was seated on it. Earth and sky fled from his presence, and there was no place for them. And I saw the dead, great and small, standing before the throne, and books were opened. Another book was opened, which is the book of life. The dead were judged according to what they had done as

recorded in the books. The sea gave up the dead that were in it, and death and Hades gave up the dead that were in them, and each person was judged according to what he had done. Then death and Hades were thrown into the lake of fire. The lake of fire is the second death. If anyone's name was not found written in the book of life, he was thrown into the lake of fire.[13]

The simple yet solemn reality of God's Word is utterly undeniable: Everyone who confesses Jesus as Lord will be forever saved, and everyone who rejects Jesus as Lord will be forever damned. In the words of Scottish professor James Denney, "If there is any truth in Scripture at all, this is true—that those who stubbornly refuse to submit to the gospel, and to love and obey Jesus Christ, incur at the Last Advent an infinite and irreparable loss. They will pass into a night on which no morning dawns."[14]

This has been the consistent teaching of the church throughout history, yet various voices under the banner of contemporary Christianity have now claimed that hell is not real—or at least not eternal. Such claims are commonly cloaked in provocative questions. *Did God really say that he would send sinners to hell? Did God really say that a person must believe in Jesus to go to heaven? Did God really say . . . ?*

Notice how questions like these are grounded in attempts to twist God's Word. We always need to be careful when someone begins a statement with the words, "Did God really say . . . ?" After all, these are the very words that caused the fall of man in Genesis 3. The deceiving serpent tempted Adam and Eve to question the love of God and doubt the Word of God: "Did God really say, 'You must not eat from any tree in the garden?'"[15] Through this question, Satan convinced this couple that God's love was subject to their own opinion and that God's Word was subject to their own judgment. He elevated the thoughts of men above the truth of God, and sin made its entrance into the world.

Let us learn our lesson here. It is a dangerous thing to twist Jesus and his Word to reflect what feels most comfortable to us. As disciples of Jesus, we must take Jesus at his Word in the context of total trust in him.

So what happens when we completely trust and carefully listen to Jesus' words on hell? Hear him describe this place of fiery agony in Mark 9:43-48:

> If your hand causes you to sin, cut it off. It is better for you to enter life maimed than with two hands to go into hell, where the fire never goes out. And if your foot causes you to sin, cut it off. It is better for you to enter life crippled than to have two feet and be thrown into hell. And if your eye causes you to sin, pluck it out. It is better for you to enter the kingdom of God with one eye than to have two eyes and be thrown into hell, where "their worm does not die, and the fire is not quenched."

As we've already seen in Revelation 20:15, God's Word tells us that "if anyone's name was not found written in the book of life, he was thrown into the lake of fire." In a similar way, Revelation 21:8 envisions hell as "the fiery lake of burning sulfur."

You may wonder, *Well, isn't fire just an image in these passages? Aren't these verses symbolic?*

Maybe.

But even if they are symbols, what are they symbols for? A wintry retreat or a summer vacation? No, these stand for something much worse. Surely burning fire and smoking sulfur are not symbols for a nice place to be. They are images that represent a terrifying place to be.

Hell, according to Jesus, is a place of conscious torment and utter darkness.[16] Later in the New Testament, hell is described as a place of never-ending destruction where people are separated from the presence of the Lord and the power of his might.[17]

Most horrifying of all, hell is a place of eternal duration. Jesus contrasted eternal punishment with eternal life.[18] John wrote about sinners in Revelation 14:11, saying, "The smoke of their torment rises for ever and ever."

In the words of Thomas Watson, "The wicked in hell shall be always dying but never dead. The smoke of the furnace ascends forever and ever. Oh, who can endure thus to be ever upon the rack? The word 'ever' breaks the heart." As people listened to Jonathan Edwards preach in the eighteenth century, they were "urged to consider the torment of burning like a livid coal, not for an instant or a day, but for 'millions of millions of ages,' at the end of which they would know that their torment was no nearer to an end than ever before, and that they would 'never, never be delivered.'"[19]

But we no longer believe in the horror of hell. Today, we say things like "We had a hell of a time" or "We played a hell of a game" or "That was a hell of a song." The way we talk about hell shows that we have no idea what we are talking about.

But we cannot be ignorant of this, and we must not be indifferent to it. According to Jesus, there is ever-agonizing, never-ending wrath awaiting lost sinners before a holy God. He has spoken. Clearly.

JESUS AND HEAVEN

Thankfully, Jesus has spoken just as clearly on heaven. He proclaims, "I am the resurrection and the life. He who believes in me will live, even though he dies; and whoever lives and believes in me will never die."[20] Indeed, Jesus says, "Whoever believes in [me will] not perish."[21] We find comfort in passages where Jesus promises his disciples that he is preparing a place for them,[22] a place where one day all who believe in him will dwell with God in "a new heaven and a new earth" where God "will wipe every tear from their eyes. There will be no more death or mourning or crying or pain, for the old order of things has passed away."[23] Over and over again, Jesus promises everlasting joy and eternal life to all who turn from themselves and their sin to trust in him.

Jesus' words about eternity encourage every person who trusts in him. Casey, a member of our church in his early thirties, once looked like the epitome of health, strength, and fitness. But one day Casey experienced some stomach pains, and after a series of tests, he was diagnosed with cancer. Weeks later, Casey went in for surgery, and when he woke up, the doctors gave him, his wife, and their precious little girl news that they never could have imagined. "When we opened up your stomach, we saw cancer all throughout your body. Unfortunately, there is nothing we can do to stop it." They continued, "You likely have only a few more weeks to live."

As Casey's death drew near, I went to see him in the hospital, and on my way I thought, *What do I say to Casey? Do I tell him I'm sorry this happened to him? That I wish this weren't the case?*

But I needn't have worried, for those who visited Casey that day were in for a surprise. Whenever anyone walked into his hospital room, Casey greeted them by pointing to heaven and saying with the sincerest of smiles, "I'm going to be with Jesus today."

All of a sudden, anything I might have said—"I'm sorry this happened to you" or "I wish this weren't the case"—just didn't seem appropriate anymore. In fact, I actually left his hospital room that day a bit envious! For that hospital room, by the power of Jesus' words, had been turned into a place for Jesus' worship, and as Jesus' disciple, this brother knew in his mind and believed in his heart that it is indeed true: "To live is Christ and to die is gain."[24]

True belief in both heaven and hell radically changes the way we live on earth. We are encouraged by the hope of heaven, and we are compelled by the horror of hell. We know that this world is not all that exists. We know that every person on the planet is only here for a brief moment, and an eternity lies ahead of us all—an eternity that is either filled with ever-increasing delight or never-ending damnation.

So Jesus' words make sense: "Follow me, and I will make you fishers of men." If you and I know and believe that Jesus came to save us from hell for heaven, then we have no choice but to spend our lives on earth making that salvation known. If the people sitting next to us at a coffee shop or studying next to us in the library or working next to us in the office or living next to us in our neighborhoods may be on a road that leads to everlasting suffering, then we *must* tell them about the Christ who leads to eternal satisfaction. Anything less than this makes no sense according to what we believe. How can any Christian stay silent and sit idly by while family, friends, neighbors, coworkers, and acquaintances walk off an eternal cliff into everlasting darkness?

So do you believe what Jesus said? Do you trust his words on hell as much as you trust his words on heaven? Has your mind—and life—been totally transformed by his truth?

BELIEVING REQUIRES PROCLAIMING

Following Jesus necessitates believing Jesus, and believing Jesus leads to proclaiming Jesus. Consequently, a privatized faith in a resurrected Christ is practically inconceivable. Yet privatized Christianity is a curse across our culture and the church today.

Multitudes of professing Christians say (or at least think), "Jesus has saved me. Jesus' teachings work for me. But who am I to tell other people what they should believe? Who am I to tell others that their belief is wrong and my belief is right? Even more, who am I to tell them that if they don't believe in what I believe, they will spend forever in hell?"

I completely understand this feeling. I remember standing one day in a sea of people in northern India. If you've never been to India, just think *people*. Lots and lots and lots of people. Approximately 1.2 billion of them, to be precise, over 600 million of whom live in northern India. Crowded streets and urban slums are surrounded by seemingly endless villages that span the countryside. Economic disparity runs rampant as more people live below the poverty line in India than the entire population of the United States put together.

But India's poverty is not merely physical; it's spiritual, as well. The church partners with whom we work in India estimate that approximately 0.5 percent of the people in northern India are Christians. In other words, 99.5 percent of the people in northern India have not believed in Christ for salvation.

Knowing this, I looked around me one day in that crowded sea of people and thought to myself, *Who am I to travel all the way over here to tell these people what they need to believe? Who am I to tell them that all of their gods are false, whether they're Hindu, Muslim, Buddhist, Sikh, or any other gods, because Jesus is the only true God? And who am I to tell the 597 million non-Christians who surround me at this moment that if they do not turn from their sin and trust in Jesus, every one of them will spend eternity in hell?*

It felt extremely arrogant, completely unloving, and uncomfortably brash to claim that 597 million Hindus, Muslims, Buddhists, and Sikhs around me at that moment would go to hell if they didn't trust in Jesus. And absolutely, such a claim would be arrogant, unloving, and brash—unless it is true.

If Jesus were just another religious teacher on the landscape of human history, offering his thoughts and opinions regarding how people should live, then it would definitely be arrogant, unloving, and outright foolish for me (or anyone else) to travel around the world telling people they need to either follow Jesus or face hell. But Jesus is indeed more than just another religious teacher, and Jesus is indeed the resurrected God, Savior, and King who alone has paid the price for sinners and paved the way for everlasting salvation, so telling people everywhere about Jesus is the *only* thing that makes sense. It is the height of arrogance to sit silent while 597 million Hindus, Muslims, Buddhists, and Sikhs go to hell. It is the epitome of hate to not sacrifice your very life to spread this Good News among every person you know and every people group on the planet.

COMPELLED BY A COSMIC SAVIOR

When you actually believe Jesus' words and realize Jesus' worth, then you understand that his aim is not simply to be your personal Lord and Savior and that his death on the cross did not revolve around you alone.

Christians sometimes say, "When Jesus died on that cross, he died just for me." Without question, there is truth here, for Jesus personally died for you and me.[25] But we must not stop there. According to Jesus' own words, he died so that "repentance and forgiveness of sins will be preached in his name to all nations."[26] Far beyond just dying for you and me, Jesus was dying to purchase people "for God from every tribe and language and people and nation."[27] Disciples of Jesus know that he is not merely a personal Lord and Savior, worthy of someone's individual approval. Disciples of Jesus know that he is the cosmic Lord and Savior, worthy of everyone's eternal praise.

So disciples of Jesus can't help but make disciples of all nations. If we truly believe Jesus' words and know Jesus' worth, then we are *compelled* to be part of this task. Together, we spend our lives telling hundreds of millions of people in America and Europe to turn from sin and trust in Jesus because he's worthy of their worship. We make disciples in Africa, where there are over three thousand animistic tribes worshiping all kinds of suspicious spirits and false gods, who do not deserve glory. We make disciples in Japan, Laos, and Vietnam, where there are 350 million Buddhists following Buddha's practices when Buddha does not merit their praise. We make disciples in India, Nepal, and Bangladesh, where there are over 950 million Hindus worshiping millions of worthless gods. We make disciples in China, North Korea, and Cuba, where over a billion people have grown up in Communist environments that deny the very existence of the God who reigns above all. We make disciples in Central Asia and the Middle East, where over 1.5 billion Muslims are following a false god. We make disciples among all of these peoples and among the toughest of these places because we know in our minds, hearts, and lives that Jesus has died on the cross and risen from the grave and that he alone deserves to be exalted as Lord.

EVERYTHING WE NEED

And when we believe Jesus' words, we are emboldened to live for Jesus' worship. Jesus has told us, "If you abide in me, and my words abide in you, ask whatever you wish, and it will be done for you."[28] This has to be one of the most astounding promises in all the Bible. Jesus just said, "Ask whatever you wish, and it will be done for you."

The key to understanding this promise, though, is understanding the setting in which it is given. Jesus had just spoken to his disciples about how he would die on the cross, rise from the grave, and then ascend to heaven. From there he would send his Spirit to empower them to go and make disciples all over the world. As they went, trusting in his word, Jesus promised to give them everything they needed to accomplish this task.

So this is not a promise upon which you or I pray for a new house or a better job or more comfort. No, this is a promise upon which you and I pray, "Lord, please give me everything I need to spread your truth from wherever I live to the ends of the earth." That is a prayer God is guaranteed to answer.

A few years ago, Heather and I traveled to a part of East Asia where very few people have ever heard of Jesus before. While we were there, Heather repeatedly shared the gospel with one particular girl named Meilin. On one hand, Meilin seemed so receptive to the gospel, yet clearly something in her spirit was still resisting Christ as Lord. Amid her many questions, we persistently prayed and pleaded for God to give us the words, wisdom, and grace needed to share the gospel clearly with Meilin.

After we had spent a couple of weeks with Meilin, it was time for us to leave her town. We had packed our bags and said good-bye to the group of people who would share the gospel there after we left. They were praying and studying the Bible just inside the home where we had been staying, and we could hear them talking while we were waiting outside for our ride.

At that moment, seemingly out of nowhere, Meilin rushed up to Heather. She pulled Heather aside and eagerly shared how she was turning from her sin and trusting in Christ. Right as Meilin shared this and Heather celebrated with her, the group inside the house behind us—who had no idea what was going on outside the house—was reading Psalm 46:10 aloud. I saw tears streaming down Heather's face as she prayed with Meilin, and I heard the group inside the house saying these words: "Be still, and know that I am God; I will be exalted among the nations, I will be exalted in the earth." Immediately, I was reminded that the Savior who reigns at the right hand of the Father is ready to give his disciples everything they need to exalt his name all over the world.

THE GRAND STORY

Disciple of Jesus, do you realize the scope of the story of which you and I are a part? We live in a fallen world of sin, suffering, and death. For centuries, all creation longed for a coming King who would conquer all of these things. That King came in the person of Jesus Christ. During his time on earth, he healed the hurting, delivered the demon possessed, gave sight to the blind, called the lame to walk, and caused the dead to live again. Then he did what no one else in history has done or will ever do again. After his heart flatlined for three days, he chose to come back to life. He rose from the grave in victory over sin, the devil, and death itself, and in the words of Scripture, "to him was given dominion and glory and a kingdom, that all peoples, nations, and languages should serve him; his dominion is an everlasting dominion, which shall not pass away, and his kingdom one that shall not be destroyed."[29]

Jesus is decidedly not dead; he is alive—and he is active. Jesus appeared to his disciples, ate with them, drank with them, and then sent them out, saying, "All authority in heaven and on earth has been given to me. Therefore go and make disciples of all nations."[30]

In other words, "Based on the reality of my resurrection and trusting the truth of all I have taught, go and tell the world."

After saying this, Jesus ascended into heaven before their very eyes, where he is now seated at the Father's "right hand in the heavenly realms, far above all rule and authority, power and dominion, and every title that can be given, not only in the present age but also in the one to come."[31]

He is not seated there simply to watch what is happening on earth. Through his Spirit, whom he sent, he is leading his people to proclaim his truth in every corner of the earth. And this is where we come in. As followers of Christ, every one of us finds ourselves on the front lines of a spiritual battle that is raging for the souls of men and women right around us and all around the world. The all-sovereign Son of God, our Savior, is above us, sitting in the seat of heavenly command with all authority in heaven and on earth. Day and night he intercedes for us, and he is committed to giving us everything we need to tell every person on the planet who remains captive to sin, Satan, and death, "There is Good News. Turn from sin and death, trust in the life-giving, grave-conquering King, and you will live with him forever."

So we go as disciples of Jesus who love his Word and trust his truth. We go not simply as men and women who at some point decided to make Jesus our personal Lord and Savior, but ultimately as men and women who at every point are devoted to proclaiming Jesus as the universal Lord and Savior. We believe him as his disciples; therefore, we obey him and make disciples.

OUR SOULS' DESIRE

Do you believe Jesus? Has your mind been transformed by the reality of what he taught? He said, "I am the way and the truth and the life. No one comes to the Father except through me."[32] He said, "God so loved the world that he gave his one and only Son, that whoever believes in him shall not perish but have eternal life," and then he said, "Whoever does not believe [in him] stands condemned."[33] Plainly put, if you don't believe Jesus when he says these things, then you are not a disciple of Jesus. Yet if you do believe Jesus when he says these things, then you can't help but to make disciples of Jesus.

The reason you and I make disciples is not because we have some superficial sense of duty. We make disciples because it has become our souls' supreme desire.

CHAPTER 5

CHILDREN OF GOD

WHEN WE RETURNED HOME from Kazakhstan with Caleb, we quickly learned that people say the strangest things when they see you with a child who is clearly of another ethnicity.

"He's so cute," people remark. "Do you also have children of your own?"

Go ahead and mark that down as phrase number one to never say to a parent who has adopted a child. Every time we're asked this, we have an irresistible urge to say, "Come in real close, because we have a secret to share. *He's ours.*"

People will also look at Caleb, realize he's adopted, and then ask, "Have you met his real mother?"

My response to that one is quick and clear. "Well, yes, I'm actually married to her. Her name is Heather."

They'll respond, "Well, you know what I mean," to which I respond, "Yes, and you know what *I* mean. My precious wife is not his fake mother; she's bona fide, real."

Others assume that Caleb doesn't know much about his family or cultural background, so they'll ask Heather and me if we're going to be intentional in teaching him about his family or cultural heritage. We tell them, "Absolutely. In fact, we've already begun. It may actually surprise you that Caleb knows a lot about his family background. He knows all about his granddad, who unfortunately he never had the opportunity to meet because my dad died before Caleb was adopted, but Caleb has plenty of pictures, he's heard plenty of stories, and one of his favorite videos to watch has been the 'Grandpa' video. In addition, he knows all about his other granddad, his two grandmas, his cousins, his uncles, aunts, great-aunts, and great-uncles. He has more family heritage than he knows what to do with."

Caleb has also learned about his cultural heritage. He's read books like *Goodnight Moon* and *Mr. Brown Can Moo! Can You?* He runs around the house saying, "Run, run, fast as you can, you can't catch me, I'm the . . ." (If you can finish that statement, it just may be that you have the same cultural heritage!) Caleb is eating his culture's foods: barbecue, mac and cheese, watermelon, and birthday cake. He even knows the music of his culture. He may not be able to recognize the Kazakh national anthem, but he loves "Sweet Home Alabama."

You see, Caleb is our son. He is not an alien or a stranger in our family. He is not somewhat Platt, partly Platt, or kind of Platt. He's fully Platt, with all that being a Platt involves (for better or worse).

These kinds of questions and comments from well-meaning people are not just potential annoyances to parents who have adopted. They are symptoms of something much deeper, for they reflect how little we understand about what it means to be adopted into a family. And if we don't understand the concept of adoption at its core, how can we realize the ramifications of what it means to become a child in the family of God?

Clearly, when Caleb became our son, it was not the end of a story. Instead, it was the beginning of an adventure where Caleb would live as our son. Today, Caleb knows that I'm his dad and he's my son—not just because of the love I showed by traveling to Kazakhstan years ago to adopt him, but because of the love I show him today. Without question, while his status in our family is based on what a judge declared years ago, his life is based on our relationship every day as we play cars, throw the baseball, run around the yard, and sing songs together.

This picture of joy in earthly adoption provides just a small glimpse of a far greater joy found in heavenly adoption. Without question, our status before God was settled at the moment we turned from our sin and ourselves and trusted in Jesus as Savior and Lord. But our lives are based on the love relationship we enjoy and experience every moment of every day as God our Father saturates us as his children with his affection. This is yet one more reason why we must refuse to settle for a hollow, distant, "I prayed a prayer however many years ago" brand of Christianity. There is so much more to being a Christian than this. As we follow Jesus as sons and daughters of God, we experience a desire for him and pleasure in him that totally transforms everything about us.

A SERVANT OR A SON?

Throughout the Old Testament, God is called many magnificent names and given numerous majestic titles, but rarely is he described as "Father"—only fifteen times, to be exact. However, when we come to the Gospels, the first four books of the New Testament, we see God described as "Father" 165 different times. All but one of these instances of God as "Father" occur in situations where Jesus is specifically teaching his disciples.

For example, in the Sermon on the Mount, when Jesus teaches his disciples to pray, he says, "This, then, is how you should pray: 'Our Father in heaven . . .'"[1] This is the first time in all of Scripture where anyone is encouraged to pray to God as "Father." The significance is astounding. Followers of Jesus have the distinct privilege of knowing, worshiping, talking to, and relating to God as "our Father."

J. I. Packer says in his classic book *Knowing God* that the fatherhood of God is central to understanding the Christian life. He writes,

> What is a Christian? The question can be answered
> in many ways, but the richest answer I know is that a
> Christian is one who has God as Father. . . . If you want
> to judge how well a person understands Christianity,
> find out how much he makes of the thought of being
> God's child, and having God as his Father. If this is not
> the thought that prompts and controls his worship and
> prayers and his whole outlook on life, it means that he
> does not understand Christianity very well at all.[2]

Or he may not even be a Christian at all. John Wesley was one of the most influential Christian preachers and leaders of the eighteenth century. He grew up in a Christian home and from all accounts lived what looked like an exemplary Christian life. Wesley was an honor graduate at Oxford University and an ordained pastor in the Church of England. He regularly visited prisoners in London and generously gave food and supplies to slum children and orphans. He was an avid student of the Bible. He prayed regularly throughout the day, fasted for up to forty days at a time, and attended multiple worship services on Sunday and throughout the week. He even went to the British colony of Georgia as a missionary to the Native Americans there.

Yet when Wesley returned to England from Georgia, he confessed in his journal that he was not a Christian. He wrote, "I who went to America to convert others was never myself converted to God." You might wonder how Wesley could do all of these things and yet not even be a Christian. Listen closely to what he wrote next in his journal: "I had even then the faith of a servant, though not that of a son."[3]

Despite everything that John Wesley was doing, he had never entered into a relationship with God as Father.

What about you? Do you know God as Father? Is your faith more like that of a servant or like that of a son? Does the thought of being God's child prompt your worship, prayers, and entire outlook on life?

THE FATHER'S DELIGHT

I think about the delight I have in my children and the delight I hope they have in me, their dad. I love being with them, caring for them, providing for them, and playing with them. When people ask me what I do for fun in my life, I point to my kids.

Periodically I take my sons somewhere for "guys' night out." We'll grab something to eat and then do something simple together before coming back home. When they were a bit younger, I was helping them get bathed and ready for bed after one such guys' night out. I was in Caleb's room about to get him dressed after his bath when the doorbell rang. Immediately Caleb, standing there with no clothes on, looked at me and said, "I'll go get the door."

Of course, I looked back at him and said, "No, you won't. Buddy, you don't answer the door naked. You stay right here while I go get the door, and I'll be right back." He smiled as I walked away.

I opened the door to find two Mormon girls standing outside our house.

"Good evening, sir," they said, "we're from The Church of Jesus Christ of Latter-day Saints."

Oh great, I thought. Whenever I have an opportunity like this, I want to take advantage of it, but the timing was obviously not conducive to my inviting these girls into our home on this night. As they continued their introductory spiel, I thought to myself, *How can I say something brief yet pointed that communicates in a kind, compassionate, and non-offensive way, "I long for you to trust in Christ alone and Scripture alone, and I really wish you would stop spreading a false gospel based on false teachings all throughout my neighborhood and the rest of the world!"*

But as they talked and I tried to figure out exactly what to do next, all of a sudden they stopped what they were saying mid-sentence, and their jaws dropped. As I saw the look on their faces,

I knew exactly what was happening. I turned around to see my son, at the top of the stairs, completely nude, dancing around in circles.

The girls smiled as they quickly figured out that this was probably not the best time for a conversation in our house, and so they left. Though I was embarrassed at the time, I take some comfort in the fact that nothing I could have said that night would have been quite as offensive as my son mooning Mormons.

It's moments like these that I am reminded of the delight that comes in being a dad. Obviously not because of what Caleb did in this instance, but simply because of the laughter, joy, love, and even challenges that I get to experience with my kids. One of the best things about being a parent is experiencing pleasure in my children.

Knowing this, then, I am awed when I read 1 John 3:1. "How great is the love the Father has lavished on us, that we should be called children of God!" John cries, "See it! See the delight the Father has in *you* and *me* as his *children!*"

The rest of the New Testament beckons disciples of Jesus to see that God our Father delights in forgiving us, providing for us, leading us, protecting us, sustaining us, comforting us, directing us, purifying us, disciplining us, giving to us, calling us, and promising us his inheritance. God on high experiences pleasure in doing all of these things for us as his children.[4]

For a time, Caleb and I were doing this thing where I would point at him across the room and yell, "I love Caleb!" Then he would look back at me and yell, "I love Daddy!"

One day we were doing this, and Caleb was laughing until all of a sudden he stopped, looked at me, and said, "You love *me?*"

I said, "Yeah, buddy, I do."

And then he asked what seems to be his favorite question: "Why?"

"Because you're my son," I said.

So he asked the question again: "Why?"

This time I thought to myself, *Now that's a good question. Out of all the children in the world, why is this precious little boy standing in front of me my son?* I thought about all the factors that had come together to lead Heather and me to Kazakhstan and all the ups and downs we experienced in the process. There were times when we wondered if we were ever going to have kids. I teared up, and I could tell Caleb was confused, wondering if he should ever ask his daddy why again. But I looked back at him and said, "You're our son because we wanted you. And we came to get you so that you might have a mommy and a daddy."

Doesn't it take your breath away for a moment to hear God say, "I love you"? To which we, in our sinfulness, must certainly respond, "Why?" And then to hear him answer, "Because you're my child." To which we ask the obvious question, "Why would I, a hopeless sinner, now be called your cherished child?" Only to hear him say, "Because I wanted you, and I came to get you so that you might know me as Father."

FAITH AND FEELING

Surely this delight is not designed to be one-sided, though. While I find great joy in my children, I trust that my children find great joy in their dad, as well. Whether it's the smile on their faces when I throw them up in the air or the speed of their feet when they run into my arms, their pleasure in me is palpable and their enjoyment of me, I trust, is evident.

Shouldn't the same be said of a disciple's relationship with God? If you are a disciple of Jesus, is there a sense of delight that characterizes not only God's attention toward you, but also your affection toward him? Is your pleasure in him palpable, and is your enjoyment of him evident?

We have already seen that when Jesus makes us his disciples, he transforms our minds to be like his. As followers of Jesus, we believe his truth and embrace his thoughts without exception. Being a disciple, however, involves much more than mere mental assent to Christ. Being a disciple involves emotional affection for Christ.

It is impossible to separate faith in Christ from feelings for Christ. Jonathan Edwards clearly points this out in his classic book *Religious Affections*. Edwards lived during a time when the church was divided between those who prioritized emotion over truth and those who prioritized truth over emotion. Various Christians and churches seemed to be getting carried away in highly emotional worship services that were devoid of the Word of God. In response, other Christians and churches claimed to hold tight to the Word of God while their worship was devoid of virtually any emotion.

Edwards, however, claimed that it was impossible to have one without the other. He writes:

Our external delights, our ambition and reputation, and our human relationships—for all these things our desires are eager, our appetites strong, our love warm and affectionate, our zeal ardent. Our hearts are tender and sensitive when it comes to these things, easily moved, deeply impressed, much concerned, and greatly engaged.

We are depressed at our losses and excited and joyful
about our worldly successes and prosperity. But when it
comes to spiritual matters, how dull we feel! How heavy
and hard our hearts! We can sit and hear of the infinite
height, and depth, and length, and breadth of the love
of God in Christ Jesus, of his giving his infinitely dear
Son—and yet be cold and unmoved! . . . If we are going
to be emotional about anything, shouldn't it be our
spiritual lives? Is anything more inspiring, more exciting,
more loveable and desirable in heaven or earth than the
gospel of Jesus Christ? . . . The gospel story is designed
to affect us emotionally—and our emotions are designed
to be affected by its beauty and glory. It touches our
hearts at their tenderest parts, shaking us deeply to the
core. We should be utterly humbled that we are not more
emotionally affected than we are.[5]

According to Edwards, faith fuels feeling. True intellectual
knowledge of God naturally and necessarily involves deep emotional
desire for God.

THE BREAD OF LIFE

But Jonathan Edwards was not the first person to point this out.
The relationship between faith and feeling, intellect and emotion,
attention and affection is clear throughout the Bible, and it's particularly poignant in Jesus' teaching in the Gospels. Consider his
words to the crowds after he fed over five thousand people with
five loaves of bread and two fish. Naturally, the multitudes around

him grew even more massive (who doesn't like free food?), and as they asked him questions, Jesus transitioned their thoughts from food for their stomachs to food for their souls. His conversation with the crowds that day led to a triumphant claim as Jesus said to them, "I am the bread of life. He who comes to me will never go hungry, and he who believes in me will never be thirsty."[6]

In these words, Jesus capitalized on the cravings of the crowds to help them understand who he was and what it meant to follow him.

We've all been created with cravings—cravings for things like air, food, water, and companionship. God told Adam in the Garden of Eden, "You are free to eat and enjoy!"[7] This garden paradise where Adam and Eve lived was not a place where humans had no needs or desires. Instead, it was a place where all of their needs and desires were met by the God who created them.

The same is true in our lives. You and I have cravings that are designed to be satisfied by our Creator. God has hardwired us with desires for water, food, friends, meaning, and purpose, and each of these cravings is intended to drive us to God as the giver of all good gifts and the sole source of all satisfaction.

Yet in Genesis 3, the cravings of humanity drove them away from God. Consider the anatomy of that first sin, and realize how much the initial sin in the world revolved around cravings, or desires. Listen to the story: "When the woman saw that the fruit of the tree was good for food and pleasing to the eye, and also desirable for gaining wisdom, she took some and ate it. She also gave some to her husband, who was with her, and he ate it."[8] Notice that the trigger of sin involved the man and woman looking to the things of this world to satisfy them apart from their Creator. For the first time in the world, the desires of humanity drove them to fulfill those desires apart from God. Tragically, in Adam and Eve's quest to feed their stomachs, they ran away from the only one who could fulfill their souls.

Centuries later, God would once again teach his people to look to him as the sole source of satisfaction for their cravings. As they wandered through the wilderness, they longed for food. In his mercy, God sent bread from heaven—miraculous manna—to satisfy his people's hunger. Each day, they had sufficient food to fill their stomachs, and in the process they were reminded that God faithfully provides for the fundamental cravings of their lives.[9]

With this background, Jesus talked with the crowds in John 6 who were craving more bread. They recounted how Moses had given them bread from heaven, and they asked what kind of bread Jesus could bring to them. Jesus' response was pointed. He said, "It is not Moses who has given you the bread from heaven, but it is my Father who gives you the true bread from heaven."[10] In these words, Jesus made clear that the bread that comes from God is far superior to the manna that came through Moses. Naturally, the crowds demanded, "Give us this bread,"[11] and the stage was thus set for Jesus' startling declaration.

"*I am* the bread of life," Jesus declared. "He who comes to me will never go hungry, and he who believes in *me* will never be thirsty."[12] In one sweeping statement, Jesus communicated to the crowds that he himself was the provision of God sent to satisfy their souls. Jesus said to the crowds, "If you want to be fulfilled, put your faith in me."

This declaration carries huge implications for understanding what it means to become and to be a disciple of Jesus. To come to Jesus, or to believe in Jesus, is to look to him to satisfy your soul forever. To come to Jesus is to taste and see that he is good and to find in him the end of all your desires. To believe in Jesus is to experience an eternal pleasure that far outweighs and outlasts the temporal pleasures of this world.

In Christ, our Creator has come to us to satisfy our desires in a way that nothing in this world can ever compare to. Now certainly this doesn't mean that every pleasure in this world is wrong. I've shared about the pleasures I experience with my family, and moments like the ones I've described are only the tip of the iceberg when it comes to all the things God has given us to enjoy in this world. Our taste buds are formed to find pleasure in good food. Our eyes are made to find pleasure in magnificent scenery. Our ears are fashioned to find pleasure in beautiful music. Our bodies are designed to find pleasure in physical intimacy with a spouse.

But amid all these pleasures we are wired to pursue, we must always remember that our deepest craving is not for something but for Someone. Our ultimate satisfaction is found not in the gifts we enjoy but in the Giver who provides them, "for the bread of God is he who comes down from heaven and gives life to the world."[13]

TRUE PLEASURE

Followers of Christ are tempted to miss this altogether. We view Jesus as the only one who can save us from our sins, but we forget that he is also the only one who can satisfy our souls. As a result, we put our faith in Jesus and trust in his forgiveness, yet we lack the feeling for Jesus that comes through fulfillment in him.

So many professing Christians think that coming to Christ involves letting go of the things in the world that we love in order to embrace things that, if we're really honest, we loathe. We may be willing to "make a decision for Christ" in order to save our skin for eternity, but truth be told, we really like the ways of this world and really want the things of this world. So we're caught in the middle. We think that we're supposed to try hard to follow Christ. Yet deep down inside, the pleasures, pursuits, plaudits, and possessions of this world seem far more enticing. Consequently, as we've already seen, the lives of professing Christians are oftentimes virtually indistinguishable from the lives of non-Christians. We claim faith in Christ, yet we are just as sensual, just as humanistic, and just as materialistic as the world around us.

But this is not the way it's supposed to be. When we truly come to Christ, our thirst is quenched by the fountain of life and our hunger is filled with the bread of heaven. We discover that Jesus is the supreme source of satisfaction, and we want *nothing* apart from him. We realize that he is better than all the pleasures, pursuits, plaudits, and possessions of this world combined. As we trust in Christ, he transforms our tastes in such a way that we begin to love the things of God that we once hated, and we begin to hate the things of this world that we once loved.

Consider how this plays out in every disciple's struggle against sin. Even though the Christian has tasted of the goodness of God, the lure of sin is still strong in the world. So how does the disciple of Jesus overcome the promised pleasures of sin? For the new Christian who has struggled with pornography, how does he now fight the lure of enticing images on a computer screen? For the prosperous Christian who has enough money to buy the bigger house and the sleeker car and the nicer clothes and the finer food, how does she resist the temptation to indulge herself while ignoring urgent spiritual and physical needs around her?

Such questions lead us to one of two answers. The more common yet most unsuccessful answer is to try to conquer sin by working hard to change our actions. Much like superficial religion, we often seek to tame our desires with a list of dos and don'ts. We do what people in every other religion in the world do, going through certain motions and concentrating on certain disciplines in an attempt to conquer sin from the outside in.

But there is another way. Instead of trying to conquer sin by working hard to change our actions, we can conquer sin by trusting Christ to change our affections. Remember the words of Jesus in John 6: "He who comes to me will never go hungry, and he who believes in me will never be thirsty." This is how we overcome the pleasures of sin: by letting Christ overcome us with the power of his satisfaction. When lust, lying, greed, possessions, or pornography promise pleasure, we fight their appeal with fulfillment in Christ. We know, believe, and trust that Jesus is better, and we refuse to give in to that sin because we have found greater gratification in our Savior. The way to conquer sin is not by working hard to change our deeds, but by trusting Jesus to change our desires.

And he does. Jesus promises abiding fulfillment to all who follow him. C. S. Lewis writes:

> If there lurks in most modern minds the notion that
> to desire our own good and earnestly to hope for the

enjoyment of it is a bad thing, I submit that this notion has crept in from Kant and the Stoics and is no part of the Christian faith. Indeed, if we consider the unblushing promises of reward and the staggering nature of the rewards promised in the Gospels, it would seem that our Lord finds our desires not too strong, but too weak. We are half-hearted creatures, fooling about with drink and sex and ambition when infinite joy is offered us, like an ignorant child who wants to go on making mud pies in a slum because he cannot imagine what is meant by the offer of a holiday at the sea. We are far too easily pleased.[14]

When Jesus transforms our desires, we realize that the problems we have with sin in this world are not because we want pleasure too much; our problems are that we want pleasure too little. It is tragic when so-called Christians live just like non-Christians, running endlessly after the next temptation, the bigger house, the nicer possession, the newer pursuit, the greater notoriety, the higher success, and the more comfortable lifestyle. Such a quest for pleasure in this world reflects a lack of contentment in Christ. Deep down inside, people seem to be afraid that if they let go of the stuff of this world, they will miss out on satisfaction in this world. But disciples of Jesus gladly leave behind the trinkets this world offers because they have found surpassing treasure in Christ. The passionate pursuit of true, deep, and lasting satisfaction always leads to Jesus.

The more Christ fulfills the cravings of our souls, the more he changes our taste capacities from the inside out. The more we walk with him, the more we want him. The more we taste of him, the more we enjoy him. And this transforms every single facet of the Christian life.

DESIRING GOD'S WORD

Consider the central role of *desire* in the disciple's life. Why does the disciple of Jesus read the Bible? Because the disciple of Jesus *wants* the Word of God.

I remember when Heather moved off to college while I was still in high school. We were technically just friends at the time, but I missed her a lot more than my other friends who had graduated ahead of me. I decided to write a letter to her a few days after she left. I am humbled as I look back at what I wrote her (for reasons you will soon see), but this is what the letter said (with a little bit of commentary in the parentheses from me as I look back at my former self):

Dear Heather,

Dude, I am so glad you called tonight.

(Dude? What kind of opening is that? I know that when you write a letter like this to a girl, you pore over every word. I have no clue what compelled me to think that the first word out of the chute should be *dude*. Apparently we had just talked, so I continued . . .)

I have wanted to call you Thursday, Friday, Saturday, Sunday, and today, but I just figured you were too busy.

(You're not supposed to say that! You're supposed to say that you have been really busy. Apparently, I was not.)

When I heard your voice, it was so awesome that I can't explain how I felt. You sounded so awesome.

(Is this not the most lame thing you've ever read? Awesome? Twice? It got worse—three pages of worse— but I'll go ahead and jump to the end . . .)

Dude, I'm not just wasting ink when I say this.

(Dude again? And I'm not wasting ink? Can you tell I had never had a girlfriend? Is it obvious?)

My life isn't the same without you around, and I miss having you to talk with and spend time with. I miss you something fierce.

(Fierce? Really? Really?)

Praying for you, dude.

(For those counting, that's three dude mentions in a total of eight lines.)

> *In Christ,*
> (Don't blame this on him . . .)
> *David*

I wish this letter were a fabrication, but unfortunately it's not. I had completely forgotten about writing it (some memories are meant to be forgotten), and the only reason I have it is because my precious wife brought it out to show me on our tenth anniversary. With tears, she thanked me for passionately pursuing her and faithfully loving her all those years before and since our wedding. These words that seem ridiculous to everyone else are priceless to her, for they reflect the intimate relationship that we share with each other.

To people who have not been born again, the words of Scripture seem tedious and dull; some, maybe most, would even call them ridiculous. But to those who are followers of Jesus, to men and women whose hearts have been transformed by the passionate pursuit and faithful love of Christ, his words are priceless. They are not merely read; they are reflected upon. They are not merely examined; they are enjoyed. They are not merely analyzed; they are applied. For the words of Jesus reflect the intimate relationship that disciples have with him.

This is how people in the Bible talk about God's Word. The psalmist David writes, "The precepts of the LORD are right, giving joy to the heart. . . . They are more precious than gold, than much pure gold; they are sweeter than honey, than honey from the comb. . . . In keeping them there is great reward."[15]

Similarly, the author of Psalm 119 says to God:

- "I rejoice in following your statutes as one rejoices in great riches."
- "My soul is consumed with longing for your laws at all times."
- "Your statutes are my delight; they are my counselors."
- "I delight in your commands because I love them."
- "Oh, how I love your law! I meditate on it all day long."
- "Your statutes are my heritage forever; they are the joy of my heart."
- "I open my mouth and pant, longing for your commands."
- "I rejoice in your promise like one who finds great spoil."
- "I obey your statutes, for I love them greatly."[16]

So what about you? Do you love God's Word greatly? When you open it up, is it like you have discovered valuable treasure? Are the words on the page the joy of your heart? The Bible is designed to be the disciple's daily bread. More important, more valuable, more treasured, and more desired than breakfast, lunch, or dinner is "every word that comes from the mouth of God."[17]

CRAVING COMMUNION

Similarly, why does the disciple of Jesus pray? Because the disciple of Jesus *craves* communion with God.

Yet we are prone to miss this. Most of us have learned to pray and think about prayer as simply asking for things. "Bless me, help me, protect me, and provide for me"—these are often the only words out of our mouths when we bow our heads. Our prayers are filled with a list of the things we need and the stuff we want. Consequently, in prayer, we're pleased when God responds like we've asked and perplexed when he doesn't.

But what if prayer isn't primarily about giving God a to-do list? After all, Jesus tells his disciples that their "Father knows what [they] need before [they] ask him."[18] Apparently, God is not up in heaven with a pen and paper waiting for us to pray so that he can find out what our needs are. Clearly, prayer involves something far deeper—and far more wonderful—than simply informing God of what he already knows.

The purpose of prayer is not for the disciple to bring information to God; the purpose of prayer is for the disciple to experience intimacy with God. That's why Jesus says to his disciples, "Go into your room, close the door and pray to your Father, who is unseen."[19] Find a place, Jesus says. Set aside a time. Get alone with God. This one practice will utterly revolutionize your life—not just your prayer life, but your entire life. For something happens that cannot be described in words when the disciple is alone with God. In a quiet place, behind closed doors, when you or I commune with the infinitely great, indescribably good God of the universe, we experience a joy that no one or nothing in this world can even begin to compare to.

Jesus promised this would be the case: "Your Father, who sees what is done in secret, will reward you."[20] This reward is deeply emotional. We express prayerful adoration to God as we experience profound affection from God. In prayer, the disciple of Jesus finds himself or herself singing with the psalmist,

> O God, you are my God,
>   earnestly I seek you;
> my soul thirsts for you,
>   my body longs for you,
> in a dry and weary land
>   where there is no water. . . .
>
> My soul will be satisfied as with the richest of foods;
>   with singing lips my mouth will praise you.
>
> On my bed I remember you;
>   I think of you through the watches of the night.[21]

Such joyful adoration of God then yields to profound sorrow over any remaining sin in the disciple's heart. No matter how small a sin may seem, we know that our Father is perfectly holy and infinitely worthy of absolute obedience, and we shudder at any way we have disobeyed his will or dishonored his name in our lives. We can identify with Ezra, who cried, "I am too ashamed and disgraced to lift up my face to you, my God, because our sins are higher than our heads and our guilt has reached to the heavens."[22]

But then, the emotional gamut of prayer swings again to surprising gratitude, for as we confess the gravity of our sin, we are reminded of the grace of our Savior. As we recall Romans 8:1—"There is now no condemnation for those who are in Christ Jesus"—we raise our heads from the shame of our sin and take our places under the umbrella of God's mercy. We are warmly overwhelmed to consider how we now rest before almighty God, clothed in the very righteousness of his Son. Regardless of the circumstances in our lives, our hearts overflow with thanksgiving, for we know where we deserve to be in our sin and we are confident in where we will one day be because of his sacrifice. So we commune with God as grateful children who love to be with their Father.

In the context of awe-inspiring adoration and affection, heartbreaking confession and contrition, and breathtaking gratitude and praise, we then cry out for God to meet our deepest needs. We share the desires of our souls, not because we're trying to give him information, but because we trust in his provision. In all of this, we realize that the discipline of prayer is designed by God for our delight and pleasure.

DELIGHT IN EVERY DISCIPLINE

Similar desires accompany every other discipline in the life of a disciple. Why do we worship God? Because we *want* God. We exalt him precisely because we enjoy him. C. S. Lewis expresses this wonderfully when he writes,

> All enjoyment spontaneously overflows into praise. . . .
> The world rings with praise—lovers praising their
> mistresses, readers their favourite poet, walkers praising
> the countryside, players praising their favourite game. . . .
> I think we delight to praise what we enjoy because the
> praise not merely expresses but completes the enjoyment;
> it is its appointed consummation.[23]

When we delight in something, we declare our delight. When we adore someone, we announce our adoration. Isn't this, then, the essence of worship—lifting up with our lips and our lives the one we love above everything else?

Why do we fast as disciples of Jesus? Because our souls *feast* on the glory of God. Fasting is an external expression of an internal reality. When we fast for a meal or a day or a week, we remind ourselves that more than our stomachs long for the pleasure of food, our souls long for the presence of God. We are satisfied in him and by him in a way that nothing in this world can compare to—not even the basic daily necessity of food. Fasting makes sense as a discipline in the Christian life only if it is connected with desire for Christ. When we fast, we say, "More than we want our hunger to cease, we want your Kingdom to come!"[24]

Why do we give as disciples of Jesus? Because we are overwhelmed with *gratitude* for what we've been given by God. As followers of Jesus, we are not forced by God to give away our resources; we are freed by God to give away our resources. We know the spiritual treasure that has been given to us in Christ, and so we are compelled to give material treasure away for the glory of Christ. In the words of Paul, "You know the grace of our Lord Jesus Christ, that though he was rich, yet for your sakes he became poor, so that you through his poverty might become rich."[25] And so, Paul says, "Each man should give what he has decided in his heart to give, not reluctantly or under compulsion, for God loves a cheerful giver."[26] A disciple of Jesus does not give because of a feeling of obligation or guilt; a disciple of Jesus gives because he or she is overwhelmed by grace.

Ultimately, why do we share the gospel? Why do disciples of Jesus make disciples of Jesus? Certainly the answer is not because we are forced to, nor is it because we are guilted into doing so. The clear and simple motivation is a disciple's passionate longing to see more and more people know Jesus. For when our thirst has been eternally quenched by the infinite goodness, greatness, grace, mercy, majesty, strength, and sufficiency of God in Christ, we will excitedly and eagerly tell all who are thirsty where they can be satisfied. Making disciples of Jesus is the overflow of our delight in being disciples of Jesus.

ENJOYING GOD AS FATHER

The central question, then, is clear: Are you delighting in God? Are you emotionally overwhelmed, even at this moment, by the thought that you are his child? Have you truly tasted his transcendent pleasure in a way that provokes you to read his Word, pray, worship, fast, give, and share the gospel, all in addition to hosts of other actions that are now compelled by affection for God?

This is the heart of following Jesus: enjoying God as Father through Christ the Son. And when this is a reality in your life, then your reason for living is utterly revolutionized.

CHAPTER 6

GOD'S WILL
FOR YOUR LIFE

A MEMBER OF OUR CHURCH named Matthew served for many years alongside Christians in one of the most severely persecuted areas of the world. Coming to Christ in this almost exclusively Muslim nation was extremely costly. Matthew told me that on the first day men or women came to faith in Christ in that country, they were encouraged to make a list of all the unbelievers they knew (which was often practically *everyone* they knew). Then they were encouraged to circle the names of the ten people on that list who were least likely to kill them for becoming Christ-followers. Out of those ten remaining names, the new believers were encouraged to share the gospel with each one of them as soon as possible. That's exactly what they did, and this is how the gospel spread in that country.

It sounds a lot like Matthew 4, doesn't it? "Follow me, and I will make you fishers of men."[1] As soon as people become followers of Jesus, they begin fishing for men.

But sadly, this is not the case for many—maybe most—professing Christians in the world. Many have hardly ever shared the gospel of Jesus Christ with even one other person at any point in their Christian life. Even for those who have shared the gospel at some point, most are not actively leading people around them to follow Jesus.

Why is this the case? Why are so few followers of Christ personally fishing for men when this is designed to be central in every Christian's life? Could it be because we have fundamentally misunderstood the central purpose for which God has created us? And could it be that as a result, we are completely missing one of the chief pleasures God has planned for us?

As Jesus transforms the thoughts and desires of our lives, he revolutionizes our very reason for living. Understanding this reality is essential to knowing and experiencing the will of God as a disciple of Jesus.

THE MOST COMMON QUESTION

What is God's will for my life? This is quite possibly the most commonly asked question in Christianity today. We have questions and face decisions all the time, and we find ourselves constantly wondering about God's will in them.

Some decisions are small and seem less significant. What book should I read this month? Where should I eat today? Should I eat in? Should I eat out? If I eat out, where should I go? Do I want Mexican? Chinese? Burgers? Italian? What do I do when my two-year-old is having a breakdown? What do I do when my sixteen-year-old is having a breakdown? What do I do when *I* am having a breakdown?

Other questions involve large, life-altering decisions. Should I date? If so, whom should I date? Should I go to college? If so, where? What should I major in? What career path should I choose? Should I marry? If so, whom should I marry? Should we have kids? If so, how many kids? Where should I live? How should I live?

We find ourselves buried under a myriad of questions and decisions, and in the middle of it all we keep coming back to one question: What is God's will for my life? What does God want me to do? How do I find God's will for my life?

We operate as if God's will were lost. And we've devised an assortment of methods for finding it.

There's the "Random Finger Method." Whenever you need to know God's will, close your eyes, open your Bible at random, put your finger down on a verse, and then open your eyes to discover his will for your life. A friend of mine in high school tried this one. He wanted a date with a particular girl, but she wasn't showing interest in him. In his struggle for guidance in how to get her to pay attention to him, he randomly pointed to Romans 8:25, which says, "If we hope for what we do not yet have, we wait for it patiently." It was like a voice booming from heaven. He had seen the light. *Just wait*, the will of God was saying, *and she will come around.* The only problem was that this verse was never intended to bring hope to a desperate teenager looking for a date. It was written to give hope to suffering people who were waiting for the day when they would see Christ. And in the end, this girl apparently didn't hear the same boom from heaven that my friend did.

So we move on to the "Astonishing Miracle Method." Look for a burning bush like Moses found or a blinding light like Paul experienced, and there you will find the will of God. The primary problem with this method is that it's apparently not too common. Among people I've asked, very few have talked with a bush (or at least a bush that talked back to them) and not many others have been blinded by a light while walking down a road. Apparently this is not God's most popular method.

What about the "Striking Coincidence Method"? This method tells us to be on the lookout for striking coincidences to pop up and tell us what we should do. Maybe you're in college and debating whether to major in English or math. You go to sleep one evening and wake up in the middle of the night, look over at the clock, and it says, "2:22." Then the next night, you wake up and the clock says "3:33." You think something is going on, so you go to sleep the next night with eager anticipation and just happen to wake up, look over at the clock, and it says, "4:44." Stunned, you get out of your bed and fall to your knees, for God has spoken. Math it is.

Or maybe God is just telling you to take some NyQuil so you can sleep through the night.

Imagine you're that same college student and you're walking down the sidewalk on your campus, thinking about the person God wants you to marry. Someone has littered a classic red Coke can, and you're kicking it as you walk. Suddenly you look up and see a group of girls standing ahead of you. In the middle of them, you see one girl standing with a bright red shirt on. You stop dead in your tracks. Yet again, the Lord has spoken. You look down at the red Coke can and then up at the girl in the red shirt and conclude that God has shown you the woman of your dreams.

Of course, at this point, you are basing your understanding of God's will and your future marriage on the idea that God caused someone to litter a Coke can at the very spot where you would be walking. And it's a good thing that litterbug wasn't a Sprite drinker, because if he were, you would have looked up and seen the girl in the green shirt, and you would have married the wrong girl and messed up your life, her life, the life of the guy she was supposed to marry, and so on—you'd have messed up the whole thing for everybody.

The list goes on. We have the "Cast the Fleece Method," which requires testing God to see what he wants us to do. We have the "Still Small Voice Method," which advocates waiting for God to speak in a still, small way, and when his voice is still enough and small enough to meet our standards (whatever those are), we know his will. Then we have the "Open Door Method," which says that if God opens up an opportunity, it is obviously his will for us to take it. Another version of this one is the "Closed Door Method": if a decision seems difficult, it's obviously not God's will for us to make it (for he would never want us to do anything difficult).[2]

With good intentions, we try hard to use various methods to find God's will. But what if God's will was never intended to be found? In fact, what if it was never hidden from us in the first place? What if God the Father has not sent his children on a cosmic Easter egg hunt to discover his will while he sits back in heaven saying, "You're getting colder . . . warmer . . . colder . . ."? And what if searching for God's will like this actually misses the entire point of what it means to be a disciple of Jesus?

THE MORE IMPORTANT ISSUE

Consider how discipleship transforms not only our minds and emotions, but also our wills. You and I have seen that when we come to Christ, we die to ourselves. To return to Paul's words, each of us says as a Christian, "I have been crucified with Christ and I no longer live, but Christ lives in me."[3] As followers of Jesus, our lives are subsumed in his life, and our ways are totally surrendered to his will.

This is precisely what we illustrate in baptism when we first become followers of Jesus. Paul asked the Roman Christians, "Don't you know that all of us who were baptized into Christ Jesus were baptized into his death? We were therefore buried with him through baptism into death in order that, just as Christ was raised from the dead through the glory of the Father, we too may live a new life."[4] In baptism the Christian makes a public declaration that he or she is dead to sin and alive to Christ. Just as Jesus died, so a disciple has died to self. Just as Jesus rose again, so a disciple now lives in Christ.

The significance of baptism was etched into my mind and heart during my time with Asian brothers and sisters in underground house churches. I was teaching one day from Matthew 28 on making disciples, and I explained Jesus' command for Christians to be baptized. I emphasized how baptism is a critical, essential, and nonnegotiable step of obedience for a new follower of Christ because it symbolizes his or her fundamental identification with the death and resurrection of Jesus.

After I finished, two of the men in the room, Li and Huan, shared that they had not yet been baptized, and they wanted to be. So the next day, one of the pastors in this house church, Jiang, asked me to do some more extensive teaching on baptism. As I walked through passages like Romans 6, it suddenly hit me. I was sitting in a country where it was illegal for these two men to identify themselves as followers of Christ through baptism. This was a decisive turning point in their lives and a potentially dangerous decision for them to make. Humbled by this realization, I closed our time in the Word with a reminder to Li and Huan that it could cost them greatly to be baptized that day.

Immediately, Jiang asked Li and Huan to come to the middle of the room. Everyone sat silently by as Li and Huan took their stand. Jiang looked at Li, a brother in his midtwenties who had just recently come to faith in Christ, and asked him point-blank, "Li, are you willing to be baptized, knowing that it may cost you your life?" With unhesitating resolve, Li looked back at Jiang and said, "I have already sacrificed everything to follow Jesus. Yes, I want to be baptized."

Huan was a teenager who had also recently come to faith in Christ. In front of the rest of this house church, Jiang asked him, "Huan, are you willing to be baptized today, knowing that it may cost you your life?" With a slight quiver in his voice, Huan looked back at Jiang and said, "Jesus is my Lord. Whatever he says to do, I will do."

With that, Li and Huan were baptized—at the risk of their

lives. As I watched these brothers identify with Christ through baptism, I knew that from this point forward, both of their futures would be completely different. They had given everything they were, everything they had, everything they would ever do, and everything they would ever be to Jesus. They had completely and gladly surrendered their ways to God's will.

Yet the picture of these brothers in a house church in Asia is so different from the way professing Christians often talk about the will of God in our culture. So often we speak about the will of God in negative terms or somber tones.

"I don't know if I'm willing to go wherever God leads," people will say (or at least think). "I'm afraid of where he might take me. What if he leads me to Africa? Or what if he tells me to downsize my home? What if he turns everything in my life upside down?" As a result, we're anxious and hesitant to say to God, "I will go wherever you lead and give whatever you ask."

But how can a Christian ever be afraid to say this to God? After all, he is our Father. If my kids were to say to me, "Dad, this week, we will do whatever you think is best for us," how do you think I would respond? Would I make their week miserable? Certainly not. I would honor their trust in me by leading them toward whatever is best for them. Now I'm not perfect, and I don't know what's best for my children 100 percent of the time. But God does. He is a perfect Father, and he makes no mistakes. He desires our good more than we do. So shouldn't we gladly surrender our will to his?

This is what it means to be a disciple. Declared and demonstrated in our initial act of baptism, we have lost our lives in Christ, and we have gladly surrendered our ways to his will.

So is this true in your life? Is your heart wholly and unhesitatingly surrendered to the will of God, no matter what it is? If not, then what might that say about your relationship with God? Are you underestimating God's care for you, as if he doesn't know what is best for you? Or are you overestimating your wisdom before God, as if you know better than he does what is best for your life?

WALKING IN GOD'S WILL

Such questions lead us to realize that far more important than looking and searching for God's will is simply knowing and trusting God. We yearn for mechanical formulas and easy answers when it comes to the will of God, and all of the methods I mentioned previously—the random finger, astonishing miracle, striking coincidence, cast the fleece, still small voice, open door, and closed door methods—are examples of this. We want to find shortcuts to the mind of God. But this is not God's design—or should I say, this is not God's will. His ultimate concern is not to get you or me from point A to point B along the quickest, easiest, smoothest, clearest route possible. Instead, his ultimate concern is that you and I would know him more deeply as we trust him more completely.

After writing *Radical*, I received all kinds of questions and comments about specific facets of the Christian life in America. People would ask me, "What does a radical lifestyle look like? What kind of car should I drive, or should I even drive a car? What kind of house should I live in? Am I supposed to adopt? Am I supposed to move overseas to a foreign mission field?"

I found these questions, though sincere and honest, to be a bit troubling. It felt like people were looking for a box to check or a criterion to follow that would ensure they were obeying God. But such questions, if we're not careful, bypass the core of what it means to follow Jesus. Outside of the commands of Christ in Scripture, we have no specific set of rules or regulations regarding how the radical commands of Christ apply to our lives. Instead, we have a relationship with Jesus.

So we go to him. We spend time with him. We sincerely listen to his Word as we walk in obedience to it. As we do these things, God leads and guides us according to his will, and suddenly we realize that the will of God is not a road map just waiting to be unearthed somewhere. Instead, it's a relationship that God wants us to experience every day. This is the fountain from which radical living flows.

Oswald Chambers uses the illustration of a man walking on a path through the woods. Chambers asks at what point that man will ever wonder where the path lies. Of course, he says, the only time the man will wonder where the path lies is when he is actually off the path. As long as the man walks on the path, he will never have to ask where the path is. In light of this illustration, Chambers writes:

> To be so much in contact with God that you never need to ask Him to show you His will, is to be nearing the final stage of your discipline in the life of faith. When you are rightly related to God, it is a life of freedom and liberty and delight, you are God's will, and all your common-sense decisions are His will for you unless He checks. You decide things in perfect delightful friendship with God, knowing that if your decisions are wrong He will always check; when He checks, stop at once.[5]

The goal of the disciple of Jesus, then, is not to answer the question, "What is God's will for my life?" The goal, instead, is to walk in God's will on a moment-by-moment, day-by-day basis.

GOD'S WILL REVEALED

The more we know God, and the more we walk in his will, the more we understand how foolish it is to think that he would ever want to hide it from us. Instead, we realize that God's desire for us to know his will is exponentially greater than our desire to know it. He desires for us to know his will so much that he reveals it to us in his Word.

God has a will, and he has made it clear. From cover to cover in the Bible, God wills to redeem men and women from every nation, tribe, language, and people by his grace and for his glory. At the beginning of history, God creates man and woman to enjoy his grace and extend his glory across the earth.[6] The patriarchs then show us how God blesses his people so that his blessing will spread to all peoples.[7] The psalmist in the Old Testament knows this is God's will, so he prays, "May God be gracious to us and bless us and make his face shine upon us, that your ways may be known on earth, your salvation among all nations."[8] The prophets echo this cry, connecting God's salvation for his people with God's will to save all peoples. The book of Isaiah ends with God's promise to send out his people to all nations to declare his glory:

> The time is coming to gather all nations and tongues. And they shall come and shall see my glory, and I will set a sign among them. And from them I will send survivors to the

nations . . . that have not heard my fame or seen my glory. And they shall declare my glory among the nations.[9]

Habakkuk prophesies the day when "the earth will be filled with the knowledge of the glory of the LORD, as the waters cover the sea."[10]

God's will to be worshiped among the nations continues into the New Testament. In the Gospels, Jesus ends his time on earth by commanding his followers to go to the nations. He tells his disciples to make disciples, preach the gospel, and proclaim his glory to the ends of the earth.[11]

The story of the church and the letters to the church in the New Testament reveal the same emphasis. In Romans 15, Paul describes the purpose of Christ's death on the cross, saying, "I tell you that Christ has become a servant of the Jews on behalf of God's truth, to confirm the promises made to the patriarchs so that the Gentiles may glorify God for his mercy."[12] In other words, Christ died not just for Israel, God's people in the Old Testament, but so that all nations might praise God for his salvation. As a result, just a few verses later, Paul describes how his will is now surrendered to God's will, saying, "It has always been my ambition to preach the gospel where Christ was not known" so that "those who were not told about him will see, and those who have not heard will understand."[13]

Peter echoes this purpose of God in history, saying that God is "not willing that any should perish but that all should come to repentance."[14] And at the end of the Bible, God's will to save men and women from every nation, tribe, people, and language is ultimately fulfilled. John writes in Revelation 7:9-10:

After this I looked and there before me was a great
multitude that no one could count, from every nation,
tribe, people and language, standing before the throne
and in front of the Lamb. They were wearing white robes
and were holding palm branches in their hands. And they
cried out in a loud voice: "Salvation belongs to our God,
who sits on the throne, and to the Lamb."

The will of God is clear from cover to cover in Scripture. From
beginning to end, God wills to be worshiped. He wills for all
people to hear, receive, embrace, and respond to the gospel of his
grace for the sake of his glory all over the globe.

Therefore, it's not shocking for Jesus' first words to his disciples
in the book of Matthew to be, "Follow me, and I will make you
fishers of men." In the days that followed, he taught them that
he "came to seek and to save what was lost,"[15] and he told them
that just as the Father had sent him into the world, he would send
them into the world.[16] Subsequently, we are not surprised when
the last words of Jesus to his disciples are, "Therefore go and make
disciples of all nations."[17]

This is God's will in the world: to create, call, save, and bless
his people for the spread of his grace and glory among all peoples.
This will is not intended to be found; it is intended to be followed. We don't have to wonder about God's will when we've been
created to walk in it. We have no need to ask God to reveal his will
for our lives; instead, we each ask God to align our lives with the
will he has already revealed.

God's will for us as disciples of Jesus is to make disciples of

Jesus in all nations. Therefore, the question every disciple asks is, "How can I best make disciples of all nations?" And once we ask this question, we realize that God wants us to experience his will so much that he actually lives in us to accomplish it.

THE PURPOSE OF THE SPIRIT IN THE BIBLE

Now you may think, *Aren't you oversimplifying the will of God? Certainly there's more to God's will than just preaching the gospel to all people and making disciples of all nations.* In one sense, the answer to that question is clearly yes—there is more to the will of God than people simply coming to Christ. At the same time, have you ever wondered why God has given us his Spirit? We've seen how as followers of Christ, God unites our lives with the life of Jesus by putting the very Spirit of Jesus inside of us. So what is the purpose of Jesus' living presence inside of us?

The New Testament answers that question in many ways. The Holy Spirit dwells in followers of Christ to comfort and convict, to give gifts, and to provide guidance. The Holy Spirit is the Christian's Helper and Counselor who opens our minds to understand God's Word and compels our hearts to offer God worship.[18] Yet amid all of these things, one overarching purpose of the Spirit seems particularly evident from the moment he first fills followers of Christ.

When Jesus promised to send his Spirit to his disciples, he said, "You will receive power when the Holy Spirit comes on you; and you will be my witnesses in Jerusalem, and in all Judea and Samaria, and to the ends of the earth."[19] Jesus had already told them to "make disciples" and preach "repentance and forgiveness of sins . . . in his name to all nations," for they were "witnesses of these things."[20] His will for their lives was for them to witness, and he would send his Spirit to enable them to follow and fulfill that will.

So what does it mean to witness? Quite simply, it means to speak—to testify about who Jesus is, what Jesus did, and how Jesus saves. Such verbal speech makes total sense in light of how we've seen the Holy Spirit at work in the Bible up to this point. A quick perusal of Old Testament instances where the Spirit of God fills various people reveals one particular purpose associated with the coming of the Spirit. Look at these six examples and see if you can identify it:

Then the LORD came down in the cloud and spoke with [Moses], and he took of the Spirit that was on him and put the Spirit on the seventy elders. When the Spirit rested on them, they prophesied.[21]

When Balaam looked out and saw Israel encamped tribe by tribe, the Spirit of God came upon him and he uttered his oracle . . .[22]

The Spirit of the LORD speaks by me; his word is on my tongue.[23]

Then the Spirit of God came upon Zechariah son of Jehoiada the priest. He stood before the people and said, "This is what God says . . ."[24]

For many years you were patient with them. By your
Spirit you admonished them through your prophets. Yet
they paid no attention.[25]

Then the Spirit of the LORD came upon me, and he told
me to say: "This is what the LORD says . . ."[26]

In each one of the instances above, the Spirit of God is associated with the spoken word. Everyone on whom the Spirit of God came spoke or prophesied the Word of God.

When we come to the New Testament, we see eight different times where Luke describes people specifically being filled with the Spirit. Look at these eight instances, and see if you recognize a common purpose in them:

[John the Baptist] will be great in the sight of the Lord. He
is never to take wine or other fermented drink, and he will
be filled with the Holy Spirit even from birth. Many of the
people of Israel will he bring back to the Lord their God.[27]

Elizabeth was filled with the Holy Spirit. In a loud voice
she exclaimed . . .[28]

Zechariah was filled with the Holy Spirit and prophesied . . . [29]

All of [the disciples] were filled with the Holy Spirit and
began to speak in other tongues as the Spirit enabled
them.[30]

Then Peter, filled with the Holy Spirit, said to them, "Rulers and elders of the people! . . ."[31]

After they prayed, the place where they were meeting was shaken. And they were all filled with the Holy Spirit and spoke the word of God boldly.[32]

Then Ananias went to the house and entered it. Placing his hands on Saul, he said, "Brother Saul, the Lord—Jesus, who appeared to you on the road as you were coming here—has sent me so that you may see again and be filled with the Holy Spirit." Immediately, something like scales fell from Saul's eyes, and he could see again. He got up and was baptized, and after taking some food, he regained his strength.

Saul spent several days with the disciples in Damascus. At once he began to preach in the synagogues that Jesus is the Son of God.[33]

Saul, who was also called Paul, filled with the Holy Spirit, looked straight at Elymas and said, "You are a child of the devil and an enemy of everything that is right! You are full of all kinds of deceit and trickery. Will you never stop perverting the right ways of the Lord?"[34]

In all eight of these circumstances where people are filled with the Holy Spirit, the result is that those people begin to speak.[35]

When the Bible repeats something like this over and over again, both in the Old Testament and in the New Testament, we are wise to pay attention. The filling of the Spirit in God's people is clearly linked to a particular purpose: the verbal proclamation of God's Word and the ultimate accomplishment of God's will.

This is exactly what we see Jesus accomplishing through his church in the New Testament. Even though Jesus ascends to heaven in the first chapter of Acts, he still continues to work. Jesus pours out his Spirit in power upon his people. He adds to the church daily those who are being saved. Jesus appears to Paul to save him and call him to spread the gospel to the nations. He appears to Peter to lead him to accept the Gentiles into the church. As Jesus is worshiped in Acts 13, he sets apart Paul and Barnabas through his Spirit for the spread of the gospel to new areas. Jesus guides his people to different cities at different times. As the gospel is preached, Jesus opens hearts to believe it. Jesus does all of these things through his Spirit in his disciples.[36]

THE PURPOSE OF THE SPIRIT IN OUR LIVES

And Jesus is doing the same thing today. Just as Jesus filled his disciples with his power and his presence to accomplish his purpose in the first century, Jesus has filled every one of his disciples today with his power and his presence to accomplish his purpose in the twenty-first century. Yet we are prone to miss this, even in the way we talk about the Holy Spirit.

I often hear Christians say, "Well, I share the gospel when the Holy Spirit leads me." As with similar statements, there is some truth here. We want to be led by the Holy Spirit in everything we do. At the same time, we need to remember that the Spirit lives in us for the explicit purpose of spreading the gospel through us. If you have the Holy Spirit in you, you can officially consider yourself led to share the gospel! You don't have to wait for a tingly feeling to go down your spine or a special message to appear from heaven to lead you to tell people about Christ. You just open your mouth and talk about the life, death, and resurrection of Jesus, and you will be carrying out the purpose of Jesus' presence in you. In other words, when you're telling others about the wonder of the gospel, you're carrying out the will of God.

I also hear professing Christians say, "Well, I don't witness with my words; I witness with my life." Again, there's some truth here: we want the character of Christ to be clear in our actions. At the same time, when Jesus told his disciples that they would receive his Spirit and be his witnesses in the world, he wasn't just calling them to be nice to the people around them. Whether in a courtroom or any other circumstance, the basic function of a witness is to speak. As we've already seen, ten out of the eleven apostles who heard Jesus' words in Acts 1 were not martyred because they went into the world doing good deeds; they were murdered because they witnessed to the Word of God.

We have brothers and sisters around the world who are imprisoned, beaten, persecuted, and killed today not because they smile as they serve people. Martyrs from the first century to the twenty-first century die because they speak the gospel. Doesn't it seem ignorant and even arrogant to say, particularly in areas where we are free to proclaim the gospel, that we will "just witness with our lives"?

God has given us a gospel to believe, a Spirit to empower, and a language to speak for a purpose—a grand, glorious, global,

God-exalting purpose that transcends all of history. From the beginning of time through today, God has been at work, drawing people to himself, and he is using us to accomplish his will.

THE DISCIPLE'S DAILY EXPECTATION

Do you believe this? Do you believe that Jesus is at work in the world around you and that he wants to use you in alignment with his will to accomplish his work?

Several years ago, I spent a couple of weeks in one city in India. The gospel partners we were working with in this relatively gospel-less city asked us to go out every single night into a popular park full of people. "We believe that God is working in people's hearts in this city," they told us, "and he wants them to know his love. God has revealed Jesus to some of them in dreams and visions. Others of them have heard a little bit about him, and they have a desire to know more." Then they said, "Your job is to go out and find people whose hearts God has prepared, and share the gospel with them." With that, they prayed that God would direct our steps to people who were open to talking about Jesus, and they sent us out.

Every night, I went into that city park full of confidence. My confidence was not based on my personality or my ability to share the gospel. Instead, my confidence was grounded in the reality that God was already working in people's lives all throughout that park. He desired their salvation and was drawing them to himself. Now that didn't mean that every single person we talked with responded positively to the gospel. But many did. We had numerous fruitful conversations about Christ, and some of the people we met eventually became followers of Christ. Along the way, I and the team with whom I served had the privilege of being part of God's supernatural work in people's lives.

Could it be that God wills for us to approach every single day like this? Maybe he is doing things we have no idea about behind the scenes in the lives of the people we work with, live around, and meet every day. Maybe God has led them into our paths so that they might hear the gospel from us. And maybe when we speak his gospel, he will open their eyes to see his glory. This certainly seems like the daily expectation of the disciples two thousand years ago.

So imagine sitting at a coffee shop today. What if God has been preparing the woman at the table next to you to hear the gospel? What if he has sovereignly arranged the circumstances in her life to set the stage for a conversation you will have with her about Jesus? What if God desires to use you, as you speak the gospel to her today, to change her life forever?

But, you might think, *it's just not that easy to start speaking about Jesus to the person sitting next to me at a coffee shop.* We all have fears that quickly rise to the surface—the fear of offending someone, the fear of saying the wrong thing, the fear of being rejected, or even just the fear of initiating an awkward conversation. Yet such fears are only a sign that we are forgetting who we are. We are followers of Christ who have been crucified with him: we no longer live, but Christ lives in us. He has united his life with ours and put his Spirit in us for this purpose. Without him, we have reason to fear; with him, we have reason for faith.

On our own, we are destined to fail. Just think about the outrageous nature of the gospel we share. We tell people that they are wicked at the core of who they are, condemned by their sin, and destined for hell. Yet two thousand years ago, the son of a Jewish carpenter who claimed to be the Son of God was nailed naked to a wooden cross, and everyone's eternity is now dependent on denying themselves and declaring him Lord, Savior, and King. At first glance, that message certainly seems like a tough sell, doesn't it? How will anyone believe it?

They will believe the gospel for the same reason you have believed the gospel: because the Spirit of God opens their eyes to see the glory of God and to receive the grace of God. For the last two thousand years, God has willed to draw people to himself through the proclamation of his Word by the power of his Spirit, and he simply calls each of us to do the same today. And when we are faithful to obey his will, he will show himself faithful to bless his Word.

THE TRANSFORMED LIFE

As Jesus transforms our thoughts and our desires, he conforms our ways to his will. I think about Luke, a member of the church I have the privilege of pastoring. I have seen God turn Luke's thoughts, desires, and will upside down from the inside out.

When Luke was in college, he found himself living the typical collegiate lifestyle. Though he had heard of God's love, he tried to drown out God's voice with alcohol as much as he could. By God's grace, it didn't take long for Luke to come to the end of himself as he realized the emptiness of the worldly pleasures he was pursuing. Luke said, "One night I cried out for God to change me through Christ." That night, Jesus saved Luke from his sin. Luke died to himself and became alive in Christ. Not long after that, he was baptized.

Immediately after college, Luke became a successful business-man with significant means. At the same time, he was growing in his understanding of what it means to be a disciple of Jesus. After a sermon one day on God's will to be worshiped in all the world, Luke wrote me and said, "David, I realize that the entire reason God has blessed the business I lead is so that I can fulfill his purpose in the world. He has blessed me not so that I can drive a BMW or live in a big house or have prestige. He has blessed me to glorify himself."

As he began to understand God's will in the world, Luke started intentionally meditating on and memorizing God's Word. He told me, "I used to not even bring my Bible to church, but now God's Word is changing my life. My Bible no longer sits in one place long, as it now comes with me to work and every-where I go. I just want to know and follow him." Before long, Luke memorized the Sermon on the Mount (Matthew 5–7). He told me, "My insatiable desire for business books, seminars, and motivational speakers has completely gone away. God has replaced that desire with a hunger for his Word. I'm now reading through the entire Old Testament. Scripture is coming alive as I begin to see the beauty of the interplay between all of the Old and New Testament. As I aggressively read the Word, I am encouraged in the Lord, and he is daily changing my desires." Luke was not just content to soak in God's Word for himself, so he began teaching God's Word in the church.

As Luke's desire for God's Word began to grow, so did his pas-sion for Christ in prayer. He wrote me about a prayer time he had with a friend named Stephen, saying, "Stephen and I prayed together this morning for the first time. Wow! I thought we were just going to get together and pray over the request list from our small group. But we never even got to it because we were so busy pouring ourselves out before the Lord. The Holy Spirit's presence was so strong it was almost overwhelming. We both looked up with tearstained faces after about an hour and a half of prayer and said, 'What in the world just happened?'" After another similar prayer time, Luke wrote to Stephen, saying, "Stephen, after you left our prayer time this Scripture came to my mind: 'Taste and see that the LORD is good! Blessed is the man who takes refuge in him!'[37] We literally tasted and saw that the Lord was good this morning." On another day, Luke told me, "We had an awesome prayer time this morning as we prayed for about two hours. It's amazing how good God is and how he longs for us to intercede and talk with him. God is birthing in me a desire to not only pray in fellowship with others but also to pray without ceasing and about all things."

Continual praying then led to regular fasting in Luke's life. He found himself desiring God in ways he had never experienced before, and physically putting aside food for a few meals served as an external expression of an internal longing inside him. Luke literally found himself feasting on God's Word.

Meanwhile, Luke's business continued to grow, and he was invited to give an address at his corporation's annual nationwide meeting. Though he was nervous, he knew that God had given him this opportunity to speak about Christ, and so he incorporated the gospel into different facets of his speech. After he finished, he sat down and a manager across the table said to him,

"Luke, I don't have a clue what you're talking about, but I want to know more." In response, Luke fully explained the gospel to this manager and everyone else listening in at his table. When he was finished, Luke asked the manager, "Would you like to turn from your sin and yourself and trust in Jesus as Savior and Lord?" To Luke's surprise, with ten other people at the table looking on, the manager said yes, and that night he became a follower of Jesus.

In the last few years, by God's grace, Luke has shared the gospel intentionally with his coworkers, and some of them have come to know Christ. Luke has also traveled overseas, where God has opened Luke's eyes to urgent spiritual and physical need around him in the world. As Luke has felt firsthand God's heart for the nations, his life, family, and business have changed. Luke and his wife adopted a child, and Luke now takes profits from his company and pours them into ministry to physically and spiritually starving men and women. Luke wants to spend his life making disciples of all nations.

The difference between the day Luke knelt before God and became a Christian and today is nothing short of radical. In the process of transforming Luke's thoughts and desires, Jesus has conformed Luke's ways to his will. Luke is basking in the Word of God and walking in the will of God, and the joy in his eyes and passion in his heart are unmistakable. Simply put, Luke loves following Jesus, and he loves fishing for men.

A NEW WAY OF LIVING

Now I'm certainly not saying that every disciple's life should look exactly like Luke's. Far from it. In his divine creativity, Christ forms us in a variety of ways to serve in different places and positions through diverse avenues.

What is constant, though, is clear. As we turn to Jesus, he transforms us. As we die to ourselves, we live in him. He gives us a new heart—cleansed of sin and filled with his Spirit. He gives us a new mind—an entirely new way of thinking. He gives us new desires—entirely new senses of longing. And he gives us a new will—an entirely new way of living.

The will of God is for every disciple of Jesus to make disciples of Jesus. None of us need to wait for still, small voices or random coincidences or supernatural signs in the sky to realize what God wants us to do with our lives. In fact, we don't have to wait at all. Just like new believers in the Muslim country where Matthew was serving, as soon as we follow Christ, we start fishing for men. And as we do, we discover the distinct delight that is found not in searching for God's will, but in experiencing God's will. Even better than this, we discover that we belong to an entire community of brothers and sisters who are all committed to accomplishing the same purpose.

CHAPTER 7

THE BODY OF CHRIST

THE ROOM WAS PACKED FULL OF PEOPLE, and the preacher held the audience in the palm of his hand. "I would like everyone to bow your heads and close your eyes," he said, and we all followed suit.

He then declared, "Tonight, I want to call you to put your faith in God. Tonight, I am urging you to begin a personal relationship with Jesus for the first time in your life. Let me be clear," he said, "I'm not inviting you to join the church. I'm just inviting you to come to Christ." As the preacher passionately pleaded for personal decisions, scores of people stood from their seats and walked down the aisles of the auditorium to make a commitment to Christ.

Yet there was a problem in all of this. These people had been deceived. They had been told that it is possible to make a commitment to Christ apart from a commitment to the church. The reality, however, is that it's biblically impossible to follow Christ apart from joining his church. In fact, anyone who claims to be a Christian yet is not an active member of a church may not actually be a follower of Christ at all.

To some, maybe many, this may sound heretical. "Are you saying that joining a church makes someone a Christian?" you might ask. Absolutely not. Joining a church most certainly does not make someone a Christian.

At the same time, to identify your life with the person of Christ is to join your life with the people of Christ. To surrender your life to his commands is to commit your life to his church. It is biblically, spiritually, and practically impossible to be a disciple of Christ (and much less *make* disciples of Christ) apart from total devotion to a family of Christians.

But so many people think it is possible—and they try to live like it's possible. It has even become a mark of spiritual maturity today for some professing Christians to *not* be active in a church. "I'm in love with Jesus," people will say, "but I just can't stand the church."

Really?

Isn't the church the bride of Christ? What if I said to you, "Man, I love you, but have I ever told you how much I can't stand your wife?" Would you take that as a compliment?

Similarly, isn't the church the body of Christ? What if my wife said to me, "David, I love you, but I can't stand your body"? I can assure you that I wouldn't take that as a compliment.

It's impossible to follow Jesus fully without loving his bride selflessly, and it's impossible to think that we can enjoy Christ apart from his body. Jesus goes so far as to identify the church with himself when he asks Saul on the road to Damascus, "Saul, Saul, why do you persecute me?"[1] Saul hadn't persecuted Christ himself, but he had persecuted Christians, so in essence Jesus was saying, "When you mess with them, you mess with me."

To come to Christ is to become part of his church. Followers of Jesus have the privilege of being identified with his family. As we die to ourselves, we live for others, and everything Christ does in us begins to affect everyone Christ puts around us. Recognizing this reality and experiencing the relationships that God has designed for his people specifically in the church are essential to being a disciple and making disciples of all nations.

WHAT IS THE CHURCH?

Unfortunately, as we have diluted what it means to be a Christian in our day, we have also skewed what it means to be a church. The majority of people in America associate a church with a physical building.

"Where is your church?" people may ask, or "Where do you go to church?" It is common today for a pastor to spend millions of dollars renovating and rebuilding his "church." Construction teams of Christians travel overseas to impoverished countries to build "churches." Planting a "church" in our day has become almost synonymous with finding or erecting a building.

We not only identify buildings as churches; we also classify churches according to the programs they offer. This church has a creative children's program, that church has a cool student ministry, these churches have great resources for married couples, and those churches have helpful group meetings for people who are divorced. Churches often revolve around programs for every age and stage of life.

Association and identification of the church with buildings and programs reflects an overtly consumer-driven, customer-designed approach that we have devised for attracting people to the "church." In order to have an effective, successful "church," we need an accessible building with nice grounds and convenient parking. Once people get to the building, we need programs that are customized for people's children, music that is attractive to people's tastes, and sermons that are aimed at people's needs. When taken to the extreme, this means that when people come to "church," they need a nice parking space, a latte waiting for them when they walk through the door, a themed preschool ministry with a custom-built slide, a state-of-the-art program that provides entertainment for teenagers, a top-notch band that plays great music, and a feel-good presentation by an excellent preacher who wraps things up in a timely fashion at the end of the morning.

But is all of this what God had in mind when he set up his church? Better put, is *any* of this what God had in mind when he set up his church? Identification of churches with buildings may seem common to us, but it's foreign to the New Testament, where we never once see the church described as a physical building. Similarly, the New Testament never once portrays the church as a conglomeration of customized programs. So much of what we associate with the church today is extrabiblical at best (it *adds* to what God's Word says) and unbiblical at worst (it *undercuts* what God's Word says).

When you turn through the pages of the New Testament, you see a very different picture of the church. Instead of a building, you see a body made up of members and a family made up of brothers and sisters who together have died to themselves and are living in Christ. Christians are joined together by Jesus' death, his Spirit, his gospel, his sufferings, and his life.[2] Biblically, a church does not consist of people who simply park and participate in programs alongside one another. Instead, the church is comprised of people who share the life of Christ with each other on a day-by-day, week-by-week basis.

This is the pattern that was set between Jesus and his disciples from the beginning. Jesus loved these twelve men, served them, taught them, encouraged them, corrected them, and journeyed through life with them. He spent more time with these twelve disciples than he did with everyone else in his ministry put together. They walked together along lonely roads; they visited together in crowded cities; they sailed and fished together on the Sea of Galilee; they prayed together in the desert and on the mountains; and they worshiped together in the synagogues and at the Temple. During all of this time together, Jesus taught them how to live and showed them how to love as he shared his life with them.

In the same way, the New Testament envisions followers of Jesus living alongside one another for the sake of one another. The Bible portrays the church as a community of Christians who care for one another, love one another, host one another, receive one another, honor one another, serve one another, instruct one another, forgive one another, motivate one another, build up one another, encourage one another, comfort one another, pray for one another, confess sin to one another, esteem one another, edify one another, teach one another, show kindness to one another, give to one another, rejoice with one another, weep with one another, hurt with one another, and restore one another.[3]

All of these "one anothers" combined together paint a picture not of people who come to a building filled with customized programs but of people who have decided to lay down their lives to love one another. On behalf of Silas, Timothy, and himself, Paul wrote to the church in Thessalonica, "We live, if you are standing fast in the Lord."[4] Paul, Silas, and Timothy had given their lives to see these Christians stand firm in Christ. Similarly, he called the Philippian Christians "brothers, whom I love and long for, my joy and crown."[5] The church is a community of Christians who love one another and long for each other to know and grow in Christ.

A DIFFERENT KIND OF COMMUNITY

This picture thus leads the church to approach community very differently from the rest of the world. Interestingly, in the Gospels, Jesus only talks with his disciples specifically about the church on two occasions. The first time is in Matthew 16, when Peter confesses Christ as Lord and Jesus responds that the church will be built on that confession. Then, two chapters later, Jesus' only other instructions concerning the church pertain to church discipline and restoration. According to Jesus, when a brother or sister is wandering into sin, caught in sin, or unrepentant in sin, then the church should confront that person and pull him or her back to Christ. In Matthew 18, Jesus outlines a process for such restoration that eventually leads to removing unrepentant sinners from the church altogether, if necessary (a process we see enacted in places like 1 Corinthians 5).

Jesus' teaching on church discipline and restoration should jump off the pages of the Bible in front of us. This is not number 100 on a list of 101 things that Jesus says we should do as his people. This is at the *top* of the list, right after the importance of confessing him as Lord. Church discipline is not supplemental for Christians; it's fundamental. Church discipline is not optional; it is essential.

Yet we treat it like it's optional. Images of holy police on the prowl looking for anyone who gets out of line convince us that this is just not a good idea. So we easily create all kinds of reasons for ignoring discipline within the church.

It's legalistic, we say. It contradicts God's grace. Don't you know Matthew 7:1, where Jesus says, "Do not judge, or you too will be judged"? Who do you think you are to point out sin in someone else's life when your own life is far from perfect? And won't people leave the church if we start disciplining disciples of Jesus? It's probably not a recommendation at the top of the church growth plans for a church to start advertising, "We're a church that disciplines sinners."

I was eating lunch with a fellow pastor recently, talking about how we were trying to implement a process for church discipline and restoration in the church I pastor, and he said to me, "I'd love to hear how that goes. Give me a call in a few weeks if you're still there."

Well, by God's grace, I'm still here, and though the church I pastor has a long way to go in fully implementing this process,

I'm more firmly convinced than ever that such discipline and restoration is essential for every disciple of Christ and every church that claims his name. Sure, if it's handled wrongly, it can become legalistic. But if handled biblically, church discipline and restoration is one of the clearest expressions of the love of God on earth.

We live in a day when it's easy, popular, and even preferred for people to sit back and say, "Well, what other people do is between them and God. Their sin is their life, their decision, and their responsibility." But aren't you glad this isn't how God responds to us? Aren't you glad that God pursues us despite our sin and pulls us away from that which destroys us? And don't we want people in our lives who will love us enough to look out for us when we begin to walk down a road of sinful destruction?

Dietrich Bonhoeffer once said, "Nothing can be more cruel than the tenderness that consigns another to his sin. Nothing can be more compassionate than the severe rebuke that calls a brother back from the path of sin."[6] In his classic book *The Cost of Discipleship*, Bonhoeffer addresses the easy believism that had run rampant in the church in his day, and he calls Christians back to what it really means to follow Christ. He writes about the preciousness of God's love, grace, and forgiveness for sinners, and he describes how these realities mustn't be cheapened by casual approaches to sin in the church. He says:

> If the Church refuses to face the stern reality of sin, it
> will gain no credence when it talks of forgiveness. Such a
> Church sins against its sacred trust and walks unworthily
> of the gospel. It is an unholy Church, squandering

the precious treasure of the Lord's forgiveness. Nor is it enough simply to deplore in general terms that the sinfulness of man infects even his good works. It is necessary to point out concrete sins, and to punish and condemn them. . . . It is essential for the Church to exercise [discipline], for the sake of holiness, for the sake of the sinner and for its own sake. If the Church is to walk worthily of the gospel, part of its duty will be to maintain ecclesiastical discipline. Sanctification means driving out the world from the Church as well as separating the Church from the world.

But the purpose of such discipline is not to establish a community of the perfect, but a community consisting of men [and women] who really live under the forgiving mercy of God. Discipline in a congregation is a servant of the precious grace of God.[7]

God is a gracious Father who seeks after his wandering children, and we reflect his grace when we care for brothers and sisters who are caught in sin.

People may reference Matthew 7:1, but we need to keep reading all the way down to Matthew 7:5. After warning his disciples not to judge "the speck" of sin in someone else's eye when that same sin is "a plank" in their own eyes, Jesus then tells them, "First take the plank out of your own eye, and then you will see clearly to remove the speck from your brother's eye." Obviously, God alone has ultimate authority to judge. Yet in Matthew 7:5, Jesus tells his disciples to remove sin in their own lives and then help others remove sin from their lives. The last thing we need to do when a brother or sister is continually walking into sin is to say, "Well, it's not my place to judge."

I know I have blind spots in my life, and I know I am prone to sin, so I have told the people closest to me, "If you see me walking into sin, caught in sin, or being pulled into sin, please don't use super-spiritual jargon as an excuse for not helping me. Pull me back!"

In 1 Corinthians 5, we learn about a man in the church who was involved in unrepentant and gross sexual immorality (he was sleeping with his mom). Paul told the church at Corinth that they needed to confront this man concerning his sin, and if this man continued to be unrepentant, he needed to be removed from the church altogether. What's particularly interesting in this passage is the way in which God holds the members of the church accountable for that man's sin. Certainly, the members of the church were not accountable for committing the sexual immorality, but they *were* accountable for not addressing it in their midst.

This clearly goes completely against the grain of the way we think. We take a much more individualistic approach to sin. "That sin is that brother's problem," we say to ourselves and each other. But that's exactly what the church at Corinth was saying, and Paul rebuked them for it. This man's sin was that church's problem.

This reality is central to understanding the beauty of biblical, Christ-centered community. In the church, we belong to one another and care for one another in such a way that we are responsible for one another. Being a member of a church means so much more than standing next to someone else and singing some songs once a week. Being a member of a church means realizing that we are responsible for helping the brothers and sisters around us to grow as disciples of Jesus. In the same way, they are responsible for helping us. We desperately need each other in the daily fight to follow Christ in a world that's full of sin.

But won't some people leave the church (or avoid the church altogether) if we start practicing discipline the way Jesus talks about? Possibly, but we need to remember that the church is *Christ's* body to grow, not ours. I can think of all kinds of things to do that will draw a bigger crowd in the church I pastor. Soften the message. Play cool, secular music. Pass out money. Do a series on sex (seems to be the new fad today). Do something innovative and catchy to draw them in. We can spend our time and resources in the church trying to do what we think is best, or we can spend our time and resources in the church trusting that God knows what is best.

I think about Jesus' words in Matthew 18 and wonder why his initial instruction concerning the church wasn't about creating an environment where people feel warm and welcome, but instead about creating a community where sin is confronted simply, openly, and severely.

Likewise, I wonder why, at the very beginning of the church in Jerusalem, God would actually execute a couple of church members on the spot for their sin. Have you ever noticed Acts 5? In the early days of the church, when it was growing like wildfire and thousands of people were coming to Christ, we learn about Ananias and Sapphira, who were struck dead for their dishonesty. Talk about discipline! God dealt directly with sin in his church, and we can only imagine the effects. You're probably not going to draw a lot of new (or old) people to your church when people are dying during your offering.

"How do you make the church grow?"

"Oh, you have God kill a couple of people during the offering. That will do it every time."

When I read this story, I can't help but think, *What is God doing? Is he trying to prevent the church from growing?*

But then I read Acts 5:13-14, and I am astounded by what it says. Right after Ananias and Sapphira died, Luke tells us, "No one else dared join [the believers], even though they were highly regarded by the people. Nevertheless, more and more men and women believed in the Lord and were added to their number." This is how God grows the church: through holiness in Christians. God grows his church by creating disciples who are serious about reflecting the righteousness of God and honoring the holiness of God.

We must not buy into the ludicrous ideas that we need to make it easy for people to join the church, hide a commitment to holiness from members in the church, or dumb down talk about the seriousness of sin in the church. If we do these things, we may draw a crowd, but we will miss the very point of the church. Anybody can draw a crowd, but the church is distinct.

All throughout history, God has purposed to raise up a people who by his grace are so holy and so pure and so abandoned in their obedience to him that they dread the thought of disobedience. A people who are so serious about sin that they help each other to avoid it at every turn because they know how dangerous and deadly it is. God has determined to display his character through a distinct people who show a watching world that he is great, holy, powerful, and pure.[8]

Some may ask, "Well, where is grace in all of this talk of discipline?" And the answer is clear: God's grace is at the heart of church discipline. As disciples of Jesus, we have died to indifference to sin in our own lives and in the lives of people we love. We know that Christ has paid the ultimate price for our sins, and the last thing we want to do is to treat his death as if it is not most precious to us. When we tolerate sin in our lives or in the church, we trample on the sacrifice of Christ. We don't just follow a Savior who pardons our sin; we follow a Savior who purifies us from sin. And we treasure his death enough to treat sin seriously in his church.

For far too long, we have disregarded Christ's commands in the name of church growth. We have ignored passages like Matthew 18, Acts 5, and 1 Corinthians 5, pretending that our catchphrases and creative programs are more effective means for drawing people to the church. As a result, the credit for growth in contemporary Christianity today most often goes to the most pioneering pastor with the most innovative church and the most appealing worship service. It is high time for this to change so that credit for growth in the church can only go to the great and holy God of the universe who displays his glory by inexplicably drawing sinners to himself through the purity of people who've been bought by his blood.

DATING THE CHURCH

The church is a community of Christians who care for one another enough to discipline one another in sin and restore one another in Christ. But if we're honest, we are extremely hesitant to share our lives like this. As a result, Christians today are slow to make any commitment to meaningful membership in the church.

When I was a junior in high school, I hadn't had much success on the relationship front. Truth be told, I hadn't had *any* success on the relationship front. Until this one girl came to a camp I attended. Word got around that she thought I was cute, and I thought, *Hmmm . . . there's a girl who thinks I'm cute. What should I do?* I started talking to her, and then I got the nerve up to ask her to go out with me and some friends. By God's grace, she said yes.

We started dating, which consisted of talking on the phone every day and spending time together in different settings, and everything was going well until one night. I decided that I wasn't up for talking on the phone every day anymore, and I didn't really want to work at this relationship. I had plenty of other things going on in my life, so I told this girl that God, my family, and my schoolwork were more important to me than her. Yes, *schoolwork*. Needless to say, my lone dating experience didn't last very long.

That is, until this girl started dating a close friend of mine. Then I thought, *What was I thinking?* Thankfully, in the days to come, I had the opportunity to get to know this girl all over again, to the point where we eventually became best friends and decided to marry each other. Ever since that conversation one night many years ago, my bride has proved very patient with me.

But what about the bride of Christ? There's a trend that has developed known as "dating the church." There's even a great book by Joshua Harris (who, by the way, has written some excellent things about dating in our culture) titled *Stop Dating the*

Church! This phrase "dating the church" is a reference to how in our consumer-driven church market we've developed the practice of hopping from one church to the next, attending this church or that church based on how we feel on that particular Sunday morning, or maybe just substituting other spiritual activities for the church in our lives. After all, we're Christians. We're a part of the church around the world. Why would we need to commit to one local church, anyway?

We date the church for a variety of reasons. We're independent, self-reliant, self-sufficient people, and the thought of mutual submission, accountability, and interdependence seems foreign, if not outright frightening. In addition, we're indecisive. We date different churches because we can't decide on the one we really like. It's a consumer mentality applied to church shopping: looking for the best product with the best price on Sunday morning. We're always looking for the better deal, which often leads to a fairly critical attitude toward the church. We can find something wrong with every church we visit, and even when we do settle down somewhere, we're ever cognizant of the things we don't like.

On the whole, we're often indifferent. Is joining and committing to a local church really that big of a deal? Isn't it just a formality, and an unnecessary formality at that? Many professing Christians simply have no idea why dating the church would be wrong and why devotion to the church would be necessary.

It seems like the church itself has contributed to this mentality, though it hasn't always been this way. There have been times in church history when membership in the church was extremely important for Christians. Today, however, scores of people would tell me that the last thing I need to be talking about in this book is church membership (assuming that I want anyone to read this book). They would tell me that church membership just doesn't mean much today. For example, one of the largest Christian denominations in the United States boasts over forty-three thousand churches with a total of sixteen million members. Yet the average weekly attendance in all of those churches together is approximately six million people. That seems like a lot of people sick every Sunday. Clearly, church membership doesn't mean that much.

In light of all these factors, a lot of people conclude that we should just do away with the whole church membership thing. But according to the Bible, this would be a serious mistake.

MEMBERS OF A BODY

All over the New Testament, the church is described as a body in which Christians are parts, or members. In 1 Corinthians 12 alone, Paul refers to Christians ten different times as members of a body: "Just as the *body* is one and has many *members*, and all the *members* of the *body*, though many, are one *body*, so it is with Christ. For in one Spirit we were all baptized into one *body*." He continues, "The *body* does not consist of one *member* but of many. . . . God arranged the *members* in the *body*, each one of them, as he chose. . . . As it is, there are many parts, yet one *body*." Then he concludes, "Now you are the *body* of Christ and individually *members* of it."⁹

At this point, you might think, *Well, of course, we're all members of the body of Christ, meaning the universal body of Christ. Everyone who believes in Christ is a part of the global body of Christ. And that's* true. Whenever we come to faith in Christ, we join with followers of Christ all over the world and throughout all history. But is that all that Scripture teaches?

It doesn't seem so. Yes, the Bible often talks about the universal church, referring to all Christians of all time. Take the book of Ephesians, for example, where Paul includes nine separate references to the universal church. He writes, "Now to him who is able to do immeasurably more than all we ask or imagine, according to his power that is at work within us, to him be glory in the church and in Christ Jesus throughout all generations, for ever and ever!"[10] Clearly, Paul is praying that God would receive glory in all believers who are united together in the church throughout all generations.

But references like this in Ephesians to the universal church are nowhere near as common in the Bible as are references to local churches. Out of the 114 times that we see the primary word for the church, *ekklesia*, in the New Testament, at least ninety of them refer to specific local gatherings of Christians. For example, the book of Acts includes the phrase "the church in Jerusalem," 1 Corinthians references "the church of God in Corinth," Galatians addresses "the churches in Galatia," and Paul writes two of his letters to "the church of the Thessalonians."[11] Other times, the Bible even talks about churches that meet in certain homes.[12] Paul writes in 1 Corinthians 16:19, "The churches in the province of Asia send you greetings. Aquila and Priscilla greet you warmly in the Lord, and so does the church that meets at their house."

These references to local churches who gather together in specific locations are especially interesting because the Bible never refers to them as part of the universal church or a section of the global church. Paul never writes "to the part of the church that meets in Corinth." Instead, he writes "to the church of God in Corinth," demonstrating to us all throughout the New Testament that believers are joined together in local bodies of Christ that are tangible, visible expressions of the universal body of Christ.

The implication is clear. Believers in the Bible were joined together into local bodies. We never once see the New Testament addressing followers of Christ who don't belong to a local church. The letters that fill the New Testament are addressed to particular people who have identified as a church in particular places. As a result, any disciple of Jesus who honestly reads the New Testament finds him- or herself asking the question, *To which local body of believers do I belong? If Paul were writing a letter to me today, which church would I be associated with as a member?*

COMMITTED TO A CHURCH

This association as a member of a local church is massively important for a Christian's life. Listen to Jesus' words from Matthew 18, which we considered earlier:

> If your brother sins against you, go and tell him his fault, between you and him alone. If he listens to you, you have gained your brother. But if he does not listen, take one or two others along with you, that every charge may be established by the evidence of two or three witnesses. If he refuses to listen to them, tell it to the church. And if he refuses to listen even to the church, let him be to you as a Gentile and a tax collector.[13]

Notice Jesus' reference to "the church." Jesus certainly isn't saying that if a believer continues unrepentant in sin, then his sin should be told to the universal body of Christ around the world. Instead, Jesus is referring to a specific local body of believers of which that brother is a part, or member.

Likewise, when Paul addresses the unrepentant brother we considered earlier from the church at Corinth, he says, "Expel the wicked man from among you."[14] Paul is talking here about removing a brother from the church, and the picture of membership is abundantly clear. A believer is either *in* the church at Corinth (as a member of that church) or *out* of the church at Corinth, and to be out of the church at Corinth (not to be a member of that church) was an extremely serious thing.

The importance of every Christian being a member of a church is also clear when the Bible talks about church leadership. In Hebrews 13, Christians are commanded, "Obey your leaders and submit to their authority. They keep watch over you as men who must give an account. Obey them so that their work will be a joy, not a burden, for that would be of no advantage to you."[15] This verse illustrates the importance of church membership on two different levels.

For church leaders, this verse is a reminder that God has entrusted certain believers into their care in a local church. This verse reminds me personally that I have an accountability before God for the Christians he has entrusted me to pastor. So who does that include? Am I accountable to God for the care of every single follower of Christ in the universal body of Christ? Surely not in the same way that I am accountable for every single follower of

Christ in the local church that I pastor. As a pastor of The Church at Brook Hills in Birmingham, I am humbled daily by the unique responsibility and accountability that I have before God to watch over the souls of the brothers and sisters who are a part of this particular church.

Similarly, from a Christian's perspective, Hebrews 13:17 is commanding followers of Christ to obey their leaders. Does this mean that every Christian is accountable to follow the direction of every Christian leader in the universal body of Christ? Surely not. This is a specific command for Christians to follow leadership in the local church of which they are a part.

That may make many Christians uncomfortable, though. *Obey my leaders and submit to their authority?* As soon as we hear "obey" and "submit," our minds wander toward images of authoritarian leaders who force their leadership upon people or abusive leaders who misuse their positions to take advantage of those they lead. The church is certainly not blameless on this level in light of seemingly countless stories of church leaders who have been caught stealing money, committing sexual immorality, or indulging their own pride at the expense of God's people. Unfortunately, it is likely that you have been affected personally by such a story.

Further, the idea of submission implies inequality in many minds. People assume that someone who submits must be inferior, and someone who leads must be superior. But this is not how Scripture views submission. The Bible talks about how the Son submits to the Father and the Spirit is sent out by the Son, but God the Father, Son, and Holy Spirit are all equal in value. Similarly, the Bible exhorts children to submit to their parents, but that doesn't mean children have less inherent worth than their moms and dads.

Instead of authoritarian abuse or gross inequality, the Bible gives us a picture of loving leaders who selflessly serve the church. Jesus tells his disciples that "whoever wants to be first must be slave of all."[16] Authority in God's Kingdom is always a servant authority.[17]

According to Scripture, church leaders are servants of Christ, and they are responsible for teaching his truth, not their own thoughts. Hebrews 13:7 says, "Remember your leaders, who spoke the word of God to you." Leaders in the church only have authority to lead inasmuch as they are teaching God's Word, and this is why the author of Hebrews says, "Obey your leaders." If leaders are teaching God's Word, then it only makes sense for followers of Christ to obey leaders in the church. In doing so, they will be obeying Christ. But as soon as church leaders begin to teach anything other than God's Word, they lose their authority to lead God's people.

Such leaders don't just teach God's Word, though; they're set up by God to show what his Word looks like in action. The rest of Hebrews 13:7 says, "Consider the outcome of [your leaders'] way of life and imitate their faith." So God has given leaders to the church not only to communicate his Word, but also to convey what it looks like in practice so that Christians have a model for what it means to follow Christ. This is why the qualifications for church leaders in 1 Timothy 3 and Titus 1 are so clear: a church leader is intended to be an example worthy of imitation by other Christians.

So is it a good thing for you and me to commit to a church under the leadership of pastors who are faithfully teaching God's Word and consistently modeling God's character? Absolutely. According to Scripture, it's necessary. This is God's good design for every disciple of Jesus.

We could continue to explore the importance of church membership in the New Testament, seeing how church members are accountable for choosing and appointing leaders in a particular local church (Acts 6:2-6), for making sure the gospel is preached in their local church (Galatians 1:6-9; 2 Timothy 4), and for sending out missionaries (Acts 13:1-3). Hopefully, however, it's clear enough at this point that the Bible is flying right in the face of American individualism and church consumerism, bringing every single follower of Christ to ask the question, "Am I an active, accountable member of a local church?"

The question is not simply, "Is my name in a church membership list somewhere?" or "Do I attend a church somewhere?" The question is, "Am I committed to a local church where I am sharing life with other followers of Christ in mutual accountability under biblical leadership for the glory of God?" And according to the New Testament, if I am casually dating (or altogether ignoring) the local church, then I am living contrary to God's design for my life as a Christian. It is impossible to follow Christ apart from commitment to a local church.

LOCAL CHURCH, GLOBAL PURPOSE

And why would we want to live the Christian life apart from the church, anyway? Sure, churches are not perfect and they have all kinds of problems, but isn't that because we're in them? If you find a perfect church and join it, be assured that it won't be perfect anymore.

If you claim to be a follower of Christ, I encourage you to consider your present commitment to a local church. Are you sharing your life with other believers in a New Testament kind of way: loving one another, serving one another, caring for one another, and watching out for one another, even to the point of disciplining and restoring one another when necessary? Are you serving Christ under the leadership of good, godly pastors who teach God's Word clearly and model God's character faithfully?

I'm humbled and overwhelmed to even ask these questions, for as a pastor I sense the weight of Christ's design for his church. As men and women die to themselves and live in Christ, God brings them together as brothers and sisters in a family of faith. This community of Christians worships with one another regularly, serves one another selflessly, guards one another graciously, gives to one another generously, and cares for one another compassionately. In such community, we find ourselves living to see each other stand firm in the Lord.

Further, as we lay down our lives for one another in the church, we express the love of Christ to people in the world. Jesus told his disciples, "A new command I give you: Love one another. As I have loved you, so you must love one another. By this all men will know that you are my disciples, if you love one another."[18] God has said that the world will recognize disciples of Jesus by their distinct love for one another. When Jesus prayed for his followers before he went to the cross, he said to the Father, "I pray . . . that all of them may be one, Father, just as you are in me and I am in you. May they also be in us so that the world may believe that you have sent me."[19]

According to Scripture, when people in the world see the life of Christ in the church, they will believe the love of God for the world. This is yet one more reason why every follower of Christ must be committed to the church: so that the glory of God might be made known to the world. And even *beyond* the world. In the book of Ephesians, which focuses heavily on unity in the church, Paul prays that "through the church, the manifold wisdom of God should be made known to the rulers and authorities in the heavenly realms."[20] God's design is to show the greatness of his character to angels and demons alike through the portrait of his church. His plan is to take men and women like you and me, who were once objects of his wrath, and transform us into objects of his affection. God brings us to life, forgiven of sin and filled with his Spirit, and he raises us up to reign with Christ as an eternal pronouncement to the hosts of heaven and the devils of hell that he is all-wise, all-loving, all-powerful, and worthy of all praise from all people for all time.

This is the ultimate reason why every follower of Christ must be a member of a church: because every disciple of Jesus desires the glory of God. You may be tempted to think, *Well, can't I live for God's glory on my own?* And there's certainly a sense in which we are intended to display the glory of God in everything we do. But the message of God's Word is that God's glory is most majestically displayed not through *you* or through *me*, but through *us*. God raises up the church and says to all creation in the heavens, on the earth, and under the earth, "This is the bride and body of my Son, bought and purchased by his blood, to be my people and receive my power and enjoy my presence and declare my praise forever and ever."

It is a privilege to be a part of the church. To come to Christ is to become a member of his community. It is biblically, spiritually, and practically impossible to be a disciple of Christ (much less *make* disciples of Christ) apart from total devotion to a family of Christians. For as Christians lock their arms and lives together with one another in local churches, nothing has the power to stop the global spread of God's gospel to the ends of the earth.

CHAPTER 8

A VISION
OF THE POSSIBLE

IMAGINE YOUR CHURCH.

Don't picture the building or parking lot, and don't envision the activities and programs. Just the people. Whether there are fifty, one hundred, five hundred, or five thousand of them, simply imagine the people who comprise your church.

People living in a world of sin and rebellion, suffering and pain. A world where over three billion men, women, and children survive on less than two dollars a day, and a billion of those people live in absolute poverty—in remote villages and city slums where hundreds of millions are starving and dying of preventable diseases. A world where billions of people are engrossed in false religions, and around two billion of them have never even heard the gospel. They are all (literally billions of people) on a road that leads to an eternal hell—suffering that will never, ever, ever end.

But you and the people in your church have been transformed by the gospel of Christ. In your minds, you know that Jesus died on the cross and rose from the grave to save people from their sins. In your hearts, you have tasted and seen that he alone can satisfy people's souls. Your wills are now abandoned to his ways, and you long to be his witnesses throughout the world. God has banded you together as brothers and sisters in a local church with a global commission: make disciples of all nations. God has filled every single one of you with the power of his own Spirit to enable each of you individually and all of you collectively to reach the world with the gospel.

So if you had nothing but people—no buildings, no programs, no staff, and no activities—and you were charged with spreading the gospel to the whole world, where would you begin? Would you start by pooling together your money so that you could spend millions of dollars on a building to meet in? Would you get the best speaker, the greatest musicians, and the most talented staff in order to organize presentations and programs that appeal to your families and your children? Would you devote your resources to what is most comfortable, most entertaining, and most pleasing to you?

I don't think your church would do these things—and neither would mine. Not if we really believed God's Word and were honestly looking at God's world.

If we recognized that there are billions of people without the gospel, many of whom have never even heard it, and if we realized that there are hundreds of millions of people starving without food and water, we would probably not say, "Let's spend millions of dollars building a house of worship."

As we've seen, the Bible never tells us to construct a house for worship. Instead, the Bible says that we as God's people *are* the house of worship. The New Testament never tells us to build a place for people to come to us; instead, the New Testament commands us to give our lives going to people.

Similarly, if we really believed the Bible, we probably wouldn't limit ministry to a team of ministers who lead the church. After all, every single person in the church is already equipped by the Spirit of God for the purpose of ministry. Why would we want to sideline the Spirit of God in the many in order to delegate the work of God to a few?

Instead, we would all go.

Every single one of us. We would scatter as rapidly as possible to make the gospel known to as many people as possible.

It would be difficult, though, and probably costly. So even as we scattered, we would gather together periodically. The purpose of our gathering would not be to soak in a show or sit in a class. The purpose of our gathering would be to share our lives—to share the hurts and joys we are experiencing as we spend our lives spreading the gospel to the ends of the earth. We would encourage one another, teach one another, worship with one another, give to one another, and sacrifice for one another, and then we would scatter again to make the gospel of Jesus known to more people. We would do this week after week and year after year, and we would not stop until the Good News of Jesus spread from our houses to our communities to our cities to the nations.

I give you a portrait of the church in its inception.

A small band of twelve men responded to a life-changing invitation: "Follow me, and I will make you fishers of men."[1] In the days to come, they watched Jesus, listened to him, and learned from him how to love, teach, and serve others the same way that he did. Then came the moment when they saw him die on a cross for their sins, only to rise from the dead three days later. Soon thereafter, he gathered them on a mountainside and said to them, "All authority in heaven and on earth has been given to me. Therefore go and make disciples of all nations, baptizing them in the name of the Father and of the Son and of the Holy Spirit, and teaching them to obey everything I have commanded you. And surely I am with you always, to the very end of the age."[2] Just like Jesus had said from the beginning, these followers would now become fishers of men. His authoritative commission would become their consuming ambition.

Not long thereafter, they gathered together with a small group of others, about 120 in all, and they waited. True to his promise, Jesus sent his Spirit to every one of them, and immediately they began proclaiming the gospel. In the days to come, they scattered from Jerusalem to Judea to Samaria to the ends of the earth, and within one generation, they grew to over four hundred times the size they were when they started.

How did this happen?

Was it because they had extravagant buildings and entertaining programs? There were none of these.

Was it because of gifted leaders? To be sure, God did appoint particular people to certain positions in the church. But the spread of the gospel in the book of Acts took place primarily because ordinary people empowered by an extraordinary presence were proclaiming the gospel everywhere they went. It was anonymous Christians (i.e., not the apostles) who first took the gospel to Judea and Samaria, and it was unnamed believers who founded the church at Antioch, which became a base for mission to the Gentile world. It was unidentified followers of Jesus who spread the gospel throughout all of Asia. Disciples were made and churches were multiplied in places the apostles never went. The Good News of Jesus spread not through extravagant preachers, but through everyday people whose lives had been transformed by the power of Christ. They were going from house to house and in marketplaces and shops along streets and travel routes, leading people to faith in Jesus on a daily basis.

This is how the gospel penetrated the world during the first century: through self-denying, Spirit-empowered disciples of Jesus who were making disciples of Jesus. Followers of Jesus were fishing for men. Disciples were making disciples. Christians were not known for association with Christ and his church; instead, they were known for complete abandonment to Christ and his cause. The great commission was not a choice for them to consider, but a command for them to obey. And though they faced untold trials and unthinkable persecution, they experienced unimaginable joy as they joined with Jesus in the advancement of his Kingdom.

I want to be part of a movement like that. I don't want to spend my life constructing buildings and designing programs for comfortable churchgoers. Nor do I want to build a Kingdom that revolves around my limited gifts and imperfect leadership. I want to be part of a people who really believe that we have the Spirit of God in each of us for the spread of the gospel through all of us. I want to be a part of a people who are gladly sacrificing the pleasures, pursuits, and possessions of this world because we are living for treasure in the world to come. I want to be part of a people who have forsaken every earthly ambition in favor of one eternal aspiration: to see disciples made and churches multiplied from our houses to our communities to our cities to the nations.

This kind of movement involves all of us. Every single follower of Christ fishing for men. Every single disciple making disciples. No more spectators. Instead, ordinary people spreading the gospel in extraordinary ways all over the world. Men and women from diverse backgrounds with different gifts and distinct platforms making disciples and multiplying churches through every domain of society in every place on the planet. This is God's design for his church, and disciples of Jesus must not settle for anything less.

A SIMPLE STRATEGY

Journey with me to a country where conversion to Christianity is outlawed. It is illegal to share the gospel with a Muslim in this Middle Eastern nation, and it is illegal for a Muslim to become a Christian. Because of this, you might expect the gospel to be silenced, but thankfully that's not the case.

A small group of Christians are making disciples and multiplying churches in this country. These brothers and sisters are not flashy; on the contrary, they're pretty plain. As they live in this country, they are simply running a successful business that employs Muslim men and women. Along the way, they are purposefully loving people and leading them to eternal life in Christ. Their strategy is simple: make disciples based on Matthew 28.

They start by sharing the gospel. Now, you may wonder, *I thought it was illegal for them to share the gospel, so how can they do that?*

Well, these brothers and sisters know that the Holy Spirit lives inside of them so that they might be witnesses, and nothing is going to stop them from speaking about their Savior. They can't help it. The gospel of God's grace is too good to keep to themselves, and they're glad to risk their lives in order to share it with others. They don't perceive this as some sort of radical devotion to Christ. They simply believe it's normal for every follower of Christ to fish for men.

Yet they are wise in the ways they share the gospel. Their goal is to sew threads of the gospel into the fabric of every interaction with Muslims. In every conversation, in every business dealing, at every meal, and in every meeting, they look for opportunities to speak about who God is, how God loves, what God is doing in the world, and supremely what God has done for us in Christ. Of course, not every conversation involves a full-on, hour-long gospel explanation. They simply try to saturate all of their interactions with various strands of the gospel, like weaving various colored threads into a quilt. Their prayer is that in time, God will open the eyes of men and women around them to behold the tapestry of the gospel, and they will come to Christ.

As I watched this "gospel sewing" in action, I was amazed at how natural (or should I say *supernatural*) "gospel sharing" could be. In casual interactions, whether at workplaces or in homes, I listened to brothers and sisters share stories about God's Son and truths from God's Word. I sat in a shop where Mark, one of the brothers in this country, was talking with a Muslim shop owner and sharing about how Jesus was working in his life and family that week. Another time, while we were waiting to eat dinner with a Muslim family in their home, I listened to Kim, one of the sisters in this country, simply share about the selfless love God has for us.

Late one night, I found myself with Robert, another brother in this country, talking with a group of men about the divinity of Christ. This is a major obstacle to coming to Christ for many Muslims, as they consider it a blasphemous and offensive doctrine altogether. I must admit that I was a bit nervous as we sat in that upstairs room at two o'clock in the morning, surrounded by Muslims I had just met, in a country where it's illegal to share the gospel, and we discussed what could be the most contentious, provocative, and even insulting facet of the gospel.

Yet these men were open to listening because of the way that people like Mark, Kim, and Robert were living their lives. Plainly put, the believers that worked together in this business had earned the right to be heard. They were honest in their work, and they honored the people with whom they worked. They cared for each other and for the people around them in poignant ways. When other employees in the business went through hard times, these brothers and sisters showed God's love. When coworkers were sick or in need, these brothers and sisters asked if they could pray for them. Most of the time, these coworkers gladly said yes. As Christians prayed for them in Jesus' name, these Muslim men and women saw a visual illustration of God's goodness that matched the continual conversations they heard about God's grace.

As a result, people were coming to faith in Christ. They would secretly pull believers like Mark, Kim, and Robert aside to ask more questions about who Jesus is and how Jesus saves. One by one, God was drawing coworkers, their families, and acquaintances to himself. Be sure that this was not easy for anybody involved. The more people came to Christ, the more at risk they all found themselves.

This is one of the things we often don't realize about persecution and the spread of the gospel. We often think persecution is horrible, and certainly in many ways it is. But persecution is often a sign that the gospel is progressing. As long as the gospel lies dormant in a country or amid a people, and as long as no one is coming to Christ, then no one cares about Christianity. It's only when the gospel spreads and people are converted to Christ that opposition begins to rise against Christianity. It makes you wonder, then: *Though we don't seek after persecution, in a sense don't we want it to come?*

Though conversion to Christianity was against the law in this country, the men and women who came to Christ were not primarily concerned about the law or the police; they were primarily concerned about the people in their homes and communities. To leave Islam in order to follow Jesus was to bring shame upon their family and their friends. As a result, new believers could be kicked out of their homes or even killed for the sake of honor.

Nevertheless, men and women who knew they would find resistance for following Jesus were still coming to faith in Christ. Why? Because they were overwhelmed by the portrait of grace, love, goodness, and salvation in Christ that had been painted by Christians like Mark, Kim, and Robert.

Further, Mark, Kim, and Robert would not abandon these new believers once they came to faith in Christ. They knew that making disciples involves baptizing them and teaching them to obey everything Christ has commanded. As a result, Mark, Kim, and Robert made it a point to teach their new brothers and sisters what it means to follow Christ and to help them obey the commands of Christ in the context of where they lived. They joined these new believers together into churches where they baptized each other. Then they began meeting together strategically to worship with one another, encourage one another, care for one another, and carry out all the other "one anothers" that we've seen in Scripture. Moreover, these new believers started sharing and showing God's grace and love to other Muslims, just as they had seen modeled for them by Mark, Kim, and Robert. Together, they began making disciples and multiplying churches in a place we might least expect and in a way for which only God can receive glory.

As I think about Mark, Kim, and Robert, simple followers of Christ living alongside one another and working to make disciples and multiply churches, I can't help but wonder, *Why don't we all do this? Why does a similar strategy not characterize the life of every single follower of Christ in the world?*

Obviously the situation and circumstances are different in each of our lives, but isn't that a good thing? What if God has placed every one of us in different locations with different jobs and different gifts around different people for the distinct purpose of every single one of us making disciples and multiplying churches? What if any follower of Christ could do this? What if every follower of Christ should do this?

SEWING GOSPEL THREADS

Why can't we all share Christ with the same intentionality as Mark, Kim, and Robert? What if each of us was purposefully sewing gospel threads into the fabric of our everyday conversations? Consider the gospel: the Good News that the just and gracious God of the universe has looked upon hopelessly sinful people and sent his Son, Jesus Christ, God in the flesh, to bear his wrath against sin on the cross and to show his power over sin in the Resurrection so that everyone who turns from sin and trusts in him will be reconciled to God forever. In this gospel, we find various facets or components that every one of us can articulate. Every follower of Christ knows who God is, what man's ultimate problem is, who Jesus is and what he has done, how someone can be saved, and how important it is for people to be saved. So let's incorporate the character of God, the sinfulness of man, the sufficiency of Christ, the necessity of faith, and the urgency of eternity into our everyday conversations. And as we thread this Good News into the fabric of every interaction we have with people around us, let's pray that God will open eyes to see the tapestry of his glory and believe the gospel of his grace.

Practically, let's speak continually to the people around us about God as someone we know, love, and worship. Instead of speaking like atheists, attributing circumstances around us to chance or coincidence, let's put God's character on display every day before people who may not yet believe in him. Let's speak about God as Creator, as Judge, and as Savior in the context of our everyday conversations.

Similarly, let's speak about the ultimate problem of man: sin.

It may not be the most effective conversation starter to walk up to a coworker at the watercooler and abruptly say, "You're a damned and dreadful sinner in need of salvation." At that moment, the only thing that person will want to be saved from is you. Many, if not most, unbelievers are offended that you would even suggest they need to "be saved." But that doesn't mean we need to hide the reality of sin in our everyday conversations. Let's speak humbly about the seriousness of sin in our lives and in a world full of evil, suffering, sickness, pain, and death.

Then let's speak clearly and compassionately about the person and work of Jesus on a daily basis. Let's talk about his life—the people he healed, things he taught, miracles he performed, and ways he served. Let's speak about his death. Do the people around you know how grateful you are for the cross of Christ? And let's proclaim his resurrection. As Christians, we talk about difficulties in this world with deep hope and unusual joy. Every trial we face, no matter how difficult, is an occasion to point people to God-given satisfaction that supersedes suffering in this life. We talk about cancer with confidence and death with delight, for we know that to live is Christ and to die is gain.

Is there anything more important to talk about than these things? Weather, food, and sports daily dominate our conversations, even with people who don't know Jesus. Surely there is a need for us to talk with these same people about things that matter forever. What could we do in our lives that would be more valuable than this? What else might we do today that would be more significant than telling others that the God of the universe loves them and desires for them to know him and be saved from their sins forever? And what could be more exhilarating than seeing a person's life altered for all of eternity right before your eyes as he or she turns from sin and trusts in Christ as Savior? For the next ten billion years and beyond, that person's life—and the lives of scores of other people he or she encounters in the future—will be completely different as a result of what you or I have the opportunity to say today.

We e-mail, Facebook, tweet, and text with people who are going to spend eternity in either heaven or hell. Our lives are too short to waste on mere temporal conversations when massive eternal realities hang in the balance. Just as you and I have no guarantee that we will live through the day, the people around us are not guaranteed tomorrow either. So let's be intentional about sewing the threads of the gospel into the fabric of our conversations every day, knowing that it will not always be easy, yet believing that eternity will always be worth it.

PRAYER AND SALVATION

As followers of Christ who sew threads of the gospel into the fabric of our everyday conversations, we look for opportunities to invite people to turn from their sin and themselves and trust in Jesus as Savior and Lord. We don't just live for people to hear the gospel; we *long* for people to respond to the gospel. Calling people to repent and believe may feel uncomfortably bold, whether you are in a Middle Eastern country or an office cubicle, but such a call is unquestionably biblical.

Remember, though, that our goal is not merely to get people to say a certain prayer. Obviously, prayer is a proper, biblical response to the gospel. In the words of Paul, "Everyone who calls on the name of the Lord will be saved."[3] In light of this verse (and others like it), many Christians have created different versions of a "sinner's prayer," which they encourage people to pray in order to experience salvation. Such a "sinner's prayer" is not inherently wrong and has been useful in many people's moment of conversion. Many preachers, from Billy Graham to Bill Bright, have used a "sinner's prayer" to lead people to Christ. Yet we must remember that more important than asking people to pray a prayer, we are calling people to lose their lives—and find new life in Christ.

For various reasons, I'm convinced we should be biblically clear, if not personally cautious, concerning the use of a "sinner's prayer." After all, a specific "sinner's prayer" like we often think of today is not found in Scripture or even in much of church history. We never see anyone in Scripture saying, "Bow your head, close your eyes, and repeat after me," followed by a specific "sinner's prayer."

In addition, it seems that the use of a "sinner's prayer" can potentially come across as unhealthily formulaic. I talk with people all the time who are looking for a box to check off in order to be right with God and safe for eternity. But there is no box. We are saved by grace alone through faith alone in Christ alone. Such saving faith is the anti-work (i.e., the "not by works, so that no one can boast" in Ephesians 2:9), and we want to be careful never to communicate that someone's work (or words) can merit salvation before God.

Moreover, I've seen the "sinner's prayer" abused across the

contemporary Christian landscape as people "pray the prayer" apart from a biblical understanding of the gospel or "pray the prayer" on multiple occasions to ensure their salvation or "pray the prayer" without ever counting the cost of following Christ. I have experienced this abuse in my own life. I can remember lying in my bed at night as a child and later as a teenager, wondering about whether I was really saved, and then thinking, *Well, I just need to pray that prayer again . . . and really mean it this time, and then I'll know I'm saved.* I have seen this abuse in a variety of settings—here and overseas, among children, youth, and adults—where people have been called upon to "pray the prayer" and "raise their hand" in ways that, despite good intentions, were theologically man-centered and practically manipulative. And I have seen this abuse in the lives of many people I pastor who prayed the "sinner's prayer" at one point in their lives and later came to realize they were not truly saved.

Finally, it seems that having "prayed the prayer" often becomes an unhealthy basis for assurance of salvation in many people's lives. Men, women, teenagers, and children are often told, "If you prayed that prayer, you can always know that you are saved for all of eternity." But a prayer someone prayed is not the best (or even a biblical) basis for assurance of salvation. According to Scripture, assurance of salvation is always based on Christ's work, not ours. Objectively, Christians look to Christ's past work on the cross; subjectively, Christians look to Christ's present work in our lives; and supremely, Christians look to Christ's unshakable promises regarding our future.[4] Our assurance of salvation is not found in a prayer we prayed or a decision we made however many years ago as much as it is found in trusting in the sacrifice of Christ for us, experiencing the Spirit of Christ in us, obeying the commands of Christ to us, and expressing the love of Christ to others. We would be wise not to give people blanket assurance regarding their eternal destiny apart from the fruit of biblical faith, repentance, obedience, and love.

With all of this said, I want to reiterate that prayer is a right and biblical response to the gospel. When sharing the gospel, it is good to invite people to call out for God to save them. But it is unnecessary (and in some ways, for the reasons stated above, unhelpful) to tell people what they must say in order to be saved. If after hearing the gospel clearly and fully people see God for who he is, their sin for what it is, and Christ for who he is and what he has done, and if they are willing to repent and believe in Jesus—to turn from their sin and to trust in him as Savior and Lord—then there are no particular words they need to recite. The Spirit of God has awakened their hearts to the gospel of God, and they are more than enabled by him to repent and believe—to cry out for his mercy as they submit to his majesty. So encourage them to do so at that moment. At the same time, be free to let them be alone with God, if that is best. In some cases, it may actually be best to encourage people to be alone with God in order that you might not unknowingly, unintentionally, or unhelpfully manipulate a decision, circumstance, or situation. As you call others to submit to the person of Christ, you can trust the Spirit of Christ to bring them to salvation.

Then, maybe most importantly, once someone repents and believes in Christ, be willing to lead that person as a new follower of Christ. Remember, our goal is not to count decisions; our goal is to make disciples.

WORTHY OF IMITATION

Disciple making involves far more than just leading people to trust in Christ; disciple making involves teaching people to follow Christ. This necessitates that we show people (particularly new Christians) what the life of Christ looks like in action. Remember how Mark's, Kim's, and Robert's continual conversations about the gospel were accompanied by clear illustrations of God's character in their lives. In a similar way, people around us long to see a demonstration of Christ that accompanies our explanation of Christ.

This is so clearly portrayed in what Paul wrote to the new brothers and sisters in Thessalonica: "Our gospel came to you not simply with words, but also with power, with the Holy Spirit and with deep conviction. You know how we lived among you for your sake. You became imitators of us and of the Lord; in spite of severe suffering, you welcomed the message with the joy given by the Holy Spirit."⁵ Paul, Silas, and Timothy had spoken about the power of the gospel with their lips while they showed the effects of the gospel in their lives. They had been intentional to lead lives that were worthy of imitation in order to share the gospel with the men and women of Thessalonica. And when people in Thessalonica came to faith in Christ, they began to follow the example that had been set by these three brothers.

This is part of what it means for us as disciples to make disciples. In our homes and our workplaces, in our families and with our friends, as husbands, wives, moms, dads, sons, daughters, employers, employees, teachers, coaches, lawyers, doctors, janitors, consultants, waiters, salespeople, and accountants, you and I intentionally lead lives that are worthy of imitation. Through modeling the character of Christ, speaking the truth of Christ, and showing the love of Christ, we commend the gospel of Christ to people around us in the process of disciple making.

In addition, we teach people to obey all that Christ has commanded us. Now some might say, "Isn't that what preachers are supposed to do?" And in one sense, the answer to this question is yes. God has clearly called and gifted some people in the church to teach his Word *formally*.[6] At the same time, he has commanded all of us in the church to teach his Word *relationally*.

In the great commission, Jesus tells all of his disciples to go, baptize, and teach people to obey everything he has commanded them. This kind of teaching doesn't require a special gifting or a specific setting. This kind of teaching happens all over the place—in homes, neighborhoods, workplaces, on car rides, in meetings, and over meals—in the context of where we live, work, and play every day. Remember the picture God gives in Deuteronomy 6, instructing parents concerning his words: "Impress them on your children. Talk about them when you sit at home and when you walk along the road, when you lie down and when you get up. Tie them as symbols on your hands and bind them on your foreheads. Write them on the doorframes of your houses and on your gates."[7] This is the picture of Christ's church that we see in Scripture: a community of faith saturating their conversations with the Word of God wherever they go—in their homes, where they work, and wherever else they walk.

ALL NATIONS

As disciples of Jesus, just like Mark, Kim, and Robert, we share, show, and teach God's Word. This is what it means to make disciples, and Jesus has told us to do this in all nations. The phrase that Jesus uses for "all nations" in Matthew 28:19 is *panta ta ethne*, which literally means all of the ethnicities, or peoples, of the world.

Many people misunderstand this verse, thinking that Jesus is talking about nations like we think of nations today. Approximately two hundred geopolitical nations exist today, but these are not the nations that Jesus is referring to. Clearly, Jesus was not talking about the United States of America because, well, the United States of America didn't exist in the first century. Instead, he was talking about families, tribes, and clans that are commonly called people groups today. Biblical, anthropological, and missiological scholars have looked at the ethnicities represented around the world today and identified over eleven thousand different people groups—groups of people that share similar language and cultural characteristics. Many of these people groups exist side by side in a single country. For example, if you go to a nation like India or even a city like New York, you will see all kinds of different people groups with different languages and different cultural characteristics living alongside one another.

Interestingly, the Bible ends with a portrait of men and women from every single one of these people groups represented around the throne of Christ, singing the praises of God. The book of Revelation envisions a scene where "a great multitude that no one could count, from every nation, tribe, people and language, standing before the throne and in front of the Lamb. They were wearing white robes and were holding palm branches in their hands. And they cried out in a loud voice: 'Salvation belongs to our God, who sits on the throne, and to the Lamb.'"[8] Earlier in Revelation, we learn that Jesus died to ransom people "for God from every tribe and language and people and nation."[9]

Clearly, the eternal purpose of God is to save people through Christ from every people group (every *ethne*) in the world. So naturally, Jesus commands his disciples to go and make disciples among every people group (every *ethne*) in the world. This is a specific command for you and me as disciples of Jesus to make disciples of Jesus among every people group on the planet.

You might wonder how well we're doing in this task. Well, out of over eleven thousand people groups represented in the world today, over six thousand of them are still classified as "unreached" with the gospel. To be "unreached" technically means that a particular people group is less than 2 percent evangelical Christian. To live in an "unreached" people group practically means that you have little to no access to the gospel, and you will likely be born, live, and die without ever hearing about how you can be saved from your sins through Christ. Over six thousand people groups comprising nearly two billion people in the world are classified as "unreached."

This is not acceptable for disciples of Jesus. Our Savior has given us a command to make disciples of every people group, and we have no option but to obey. Nor would we want to take any other option. We who have the life of Christ yearn to spread the love of Christ.

PRAYING, GIVING, GOING

So we pray. We cry, "'Our Father in heaven, hallowed be your name, your kingdom come, your will be done on earth as it is in heaven.'[10] Cause your name to be praised and your Kingdom to spread among all the peoples of the earth." Let's pray for disciples to be made and churches to be multiplied among Saudi Arabs and Iranian Turks and the Lohar of South Asia and the Somalis of North Africa and the Brahman of India and six thousand other people groups like them.

We pray, and we give. Researchers estimate that Christians in North America give an average of 2.5 percent of their income to a local church (which I think is probably a generous estimate, but we'll go with it).[11] These local churches then give an average of about 2 percent of those funds to the spread of the gospel overseas. In other words, for every one hundred dollars that a professing Christian makes in North America, he or she gives five cents through the local church to the rest of the world.

Simply put, this cannot be the case among authentic followers of Jesus. Not only have we been spiritually saved from our sins, but we have been materially entrusted with great wealth. In the words of Steve Corbett and Brian Fikkert, "The Bible's teachings should cut to the heart of North American Christians. By any measure, we are the richest people ever to walk on planet Earth."[12]

Why are we so wealthy? I'm convinced Psalm 67 is the answer: "The land will yield its harvest, and God, our God, will bless us . . . and all the ends of the earth will fear him."[13] God has given his people worldly wealth for one purpose: the spread of his worldwide worship. Disciples of Jesus live simply and give sacrificially because we want the glory of Christ in all nations more than we want nicer comforts, newer possessions, and greater luxuries.

We pray, we give, and we go in a variety of different ways through a variety of different avenues to a variety of different peoples. We go for a week or two at a time to partner wisely with long-term disciple makers and long-term disciple-making processes around the world. Almost every week, teams of brothers and sisters are going out from our faith family into different places and among different people groups around the world to share and show the love of Christ.

One of those teams recently returned from the largest unevangelized island in the world. Almost fifty different people groups live on this island, most with no churches among them. Millions of people there have never met a Christian or heard of Christ.

So we sent a team to work with the few Christians on that island, and they hiked with a couple of translators into remote villages among one particular unreached people group. As they hiked, they prayed, asking God to do what he did in Lydia's life: sovereignly open somebody's heart to believe.[14] And that's exactly what God did. Our team shared the gospel with a household in this remote village on one of the most unevangelized islands on earth, and upon first hearing of Christ, the family in that household believed in Christ. Christians on the island have since followed up, and a church has now begun in that village. Our team came back rejoicing that they had the privilege of being a part of leading the first believers in a people group to faith in Christ.

When we start getting in on God's global plan like that, we'll want more. So let's go, as the Lord leads, for longer periods of time, whether that's two months or two years. From the church, let's send disciples of Jesus all around the world as they finish high school, study in college, finish college, and face retirement. A couple of times a year, our church sends out many members who fall into these categories.

Some may go for a week or two, others may go for a year or two, and many may go permanently. As the Spirit leads, disciples of Jesus pack their bags, sell their possessions, and move overseas to plant their lives among unreached people groups. Some of them may be pastors or missionaries with particular training for global ministry, and this is great. Yet I'm convinced that a massive force is waiting to be unleashed among disciples of Jesus in various domains of society who will simply start looking for work around the world.

God has given us access in North America to education, training, and skill development in so many different fields—medicine, business, sports, education, engineering—and all are useful in countries around the world. What would happen if disciples of Jesus stopped assuming that the default for where we might live and work is in North America? What if we began to look intentionally for jobs among the nations? What if students in the church began studying specifically for the purpose of getting jobs overseas among unreached peoples? Or what if those same students simply started studying overseas for the explicit purpose of making disciples in unreached areas? Similarly, what if business leaders began strategically looking for avenues to expand their influence among unreached nations? Ultimately, what if followers of Christ started leaving work in places where the most number of Christians live and started looking for work in places where the least number of Christians live?

I think about one couple in our church, Jim and Alicia. Jim is a businessman, and Alicia is a schoolteacher. As a result of seeing and sensing God's passion for his glory among the nations, they looked at each other one day and said, "Can't we do business and teach school among people who have no access to the gospel in the same way we do business and teach school among people who have abundant access to the gospel?" Realizing how much sense this made, they decided to move to Asia, where they are now making disciples as a businessman and a schoolteacher among an unreached people group.

Who can imagine what might happen if—or when—multitudes of disciple-making Christians truly see and sense God's passion for his glory among all peoples? This was the heart of the Moravian movement, literally centuries before the advent of the technological age and the globalization of the world. One out of every sixty Moravian believers left their home country to spread the gospel among the nations. Almost all of them were self-supported, meaning they worked in their various trades while they made disciples in various countries.

One historian says, "The most important contribution of the Moravians was their emphasis that every Christian is a missionary and should witness through his daily vocation. If the example of the Moravians had been studied more carefully by other Christians, it is possible that the businessman might have retained his honored place within the expanding Christian world mission."[15] As a result of this massive mobilization of ordinary men and women in the church, the Moravians sent out more missionaries in two decades than all Protestants combined had sent out in the previous two centuries.

Could this happen today? If we truly recognized that every disciple is a disciple maker, and if we actually realized that Jesus has commanded us specifically to make disciples among every people group in the world, couldn't we blow the lid off the number of Christians going out from our churches around the world? As long as we limit the people we send overseas to trained pastors and traditional missionaries, we will continue to see a tepid advance of the gospel to the unreached. But what might happen if students, singles, couples, families, and senior adults took their gifts, skills, passions, and training and fanned out among the nations for the sake of God's fame? Might we see the accomplishment of the great commission—disciples made and churches multiplied in every nation—in our day?

WHAT IF WE REALLY DID THIS?

Never underestimate the effect of disciples who are making disciples. As I finish this chapter, I am in India, where I just spent time with two brothers in Christ named Anil and Hari, along with their families. They live in one of the most physically impoverished and spiritually desolate places in the world. Their state is home to the poorest of the poor in India, and approximately five thousand people die in their region every day. Anil and Hari estimate that about 0.1 percent of people in their state are evangelical Christians. Based upon the truth of God's Word, that means approximately 4,995 people around Anil and Hari plunge into everlasting torment every single day.

Anil works as a school superintendent, and Hari is a chicken farmer. Though they love their jobs, their deepest passion is declaring the gospel to people around them. But three years ago, they were struggling in their faith. Facing resistance to the gospel on all sides, they wondered if anyone around them would ever come to faith in Christ.

One day, though, Anil and Hari went to a conference where they were freshly challenged to make disciples. They were encouraged to find a completely unreached village (i.e., no church or Christians among them), walk into that village, and say to anyone they met, "We are here in the name of Jesus, and we would like to pray for you and your home." Anil and Hari thought it was a crazy idea and that it would never work, but they were at the end of their rope, so they decided to try it.

At the first village Anil and Hari entered, a man approached them, and Anil began his scripted introduction: "I am here in the name of Jesus . . ." Before Anil could finish the rest of what he was saying, the man interrupted him and said, "Jesus? I have heard a little about him. Can you tell me more?"

Anil was shocked. He looked at Hari, then looked at the man, and he said, "We would love to tell you more."

The man replied, "Well, wait a moment. I'd like to get my family and some friends to hear what you have to say."

Dumbfounded, Anil and Hari walked with the man to his home, and within a matter of minutes, a variety of villagers had gathered together there. Anil and Hari shared the gospel, and the people said they wanted to hear more. Within a few weeks, twenty of them had become followers of Christ.

But the story does not end there. Anil and Hari encouraged those twenty people to find villages where they could do the same thing Anil and Hari had done. This educator and this chicken farmer took time to make disciples among a few people, who then spread to other villages to make disciples, who then spread to other villages to make disciples. As a result, since that day three years ago, approximately three hundred fifty churches have been planted in three hundred fifty different villages where there was no church before.

Who can imagine or measure what might happen when all the people of God begin to prayerfully, humbly, simply, and intentionally make disciples? What if every one of us as followers of Christ really started fishing for men? This is *the* way that God has designed for his unfathomable grace to spread to the ends of the earth for his ultimate glory. And this is *the* life that God has ordained for every child of his—to enjoy his grace as we extend his glory to every group of people in the world.

CHAPTER 9

BORN TO REPRODUCE

ONE OF THE MOST INFLUENTIAL THINGS I have ever read is a little booklet called "Born to Reproduce" by Dawson Trotman. As a college student, I walked into a Christian bookstore, and a man I hardly knew stopped me, handed me what looked like a leaflet, and said, "You need to read this." I did, and it changed my life.

In a matter of only a few pages, Trotman builds the case that "every person who is born into God's family is to multiply." Yet he maintains that most Christians are not multiplying. He laments, "In every Christian audience, I am sure there are men and women who have been Christians for five, ten or twenty years but who do not know of one person who is living for Jesus Christ today because of them."[1] This is a problem, Trotman says, and it's the reason the gospel has not yet spread to the nations today.

In contrast, "the Gospel spread to the known world during the first century without radio, television, or the printing press, because [the early church] produced [Christians] who were *reproducing*." Trotman uses the illustration of how parents naturally reproduce children in the context of marriage to assert that "every one of [God's] children ought to be a reproducer."[2]

That illustration became all the more clear to me in the years to come. I've written with great delight about my family's adoption journey, but that journey was born in dark and difficult days. For years my wife and I tried to have children biologically. Finally convinced that this would never happen, we began the process of adopting Caleb. Then, about two weeks after we returned from Kazakhstan, I came home from a meeting late one night and found Heather still awake. That was unusual.

"Is everything okay?" I asked her.

"You need to sit down," she replied.

Worried, I sat on the couch next to her and waited.

She looked at me and slowly said two shocking words: "I'm pregnant."

I was stunned. After years and years of trying, we didn't think this could happen, and we certainly hadn't planned on it. Apparently, what happens in Kazakhstan *doesn't* stay in Kazakhstan. (Did I just write that?)

Nine months later, Heather woke me up in the middle of the night. She said, "It's probably a false alarm, but I think we should go to the hospital."

On that cold December night, we arrived at the hospital, and they told us they didn't have enough room for us. *Kind of appropriate for the season*, I thought—getting ready to have a baby at Christmastime and being told there's no room. *All right . . . maybe we'll just go outside and look for a stable with a manger.*

So the hospital staff put us in a closet and hooked Heather up to all kinds of machines. A couple of hours later they were able to move us into a regular room. As we settled into the hospital, my excitement was tempered with tension. Simply put, I'm not a big fan of hospitals. The sight of blood doesn't sit well with me. Heather knows this, so I wasn't surprised a little later when I overheard her talking with our nurse.

The nurse first said to Heather, "The doctor who is going to be delivering your baby lets husbands help deliver, if they'd like."

Heather laughed. "My husband would never do that."

Wounded in my pride, I realized this was my chance to show my wife what I was made of. Before I knew what I was saying, I blurted out, "I'd love to help deliver the baby."

Heather looked back at me with a sudden smile on her face. "You would?"

"Yes . . . of course," I stammered. "Who wouldn't want to deliver a baby?"

The nurse immediately went into action, making preparations for the delivery as Heather sat back in her bed, still smiling. Meanwhile, I was sweating. *What was I thinking? I can't stand the sight of blood—I already feel sick just standing in this room—and I just volunteered to deliver a baby?*

I needed a plan, so I decided I was going to look at this as if it were a mission trip. When you go overseas, you do things you don't normally do. You eat things you don't normally eat and drink things you don't normally drink. *When you're in Rome, you do what the Romans do,* I thought to myself. *So when you're in the hospital, you do what doctors do.*

Besides, I have a doctorate, I reasoned. *Granted, it's from a seminary, but what difference does that really make? In the end, aren't all doctors pretty much the same?*

I paced until the real doctor came in. It was time. As I put on a gown and some gloves, the doctor pulled me aside and told me how this was going to work. He used a bunch of medical jargon that I didn't understand and then asked me, "Do you understand?"

Without hesitation, I responded, "Yes, sir."

The reality? I was scared out of my mind and sick to my stomach.

I'll spare you the details, but after a few minutes, he gave me the cue. He told me to reach down and put my left hand under my right hand. I felt like Peyton Manning. Flanked by two nurses, I stood waiting for the ball to be snapped.

All of a sudden, a tiny head popped out—and time stood still. I pulled out Joshua, a child we had prayed for over many years, and I placed him in my precious wife's lap while Caleb, our first son, waited in the room outside. Clearly, we couldn't have written this script. Only God, in his creative mercy and sovereign wisdom, could have designed this story—a story whose plot has since thickened. Years after Joshua was born, Heather and I adopted our daughter, Mara Ruth, from China. Three months later, you'll never guess what happened. To our surprise, Heather was pregnant again.

Looking back on years of infertility, Heather and I remember the hurts and heartaches of longing to have children yet finding those longings go unfulfilled with every passing month. We constantly felt the frustration that comes with realizing there was something physically wrong that prevented this blessing.

The Lord used this lesson to teach me, though, and today I am convinced that a similar thing can be said of the Christian life. By God's design, he has wired his children for spiritual reproduction. He has woven into the fabric of every single Christian's DNA a desire and ability to reproduce. More than any married couple longs to see a baby naturally born, every Christian longs to see sinners supernaturally saved. All who know the love of Christ yearn to multiply the life of Christ. God has formed, fashioned, and even filled Christians with his own Spirit for this very purpose.

I think, then, it's reasonable to conclude that something is spiritually wrong at the core of a Christian if his or her relationship with Christ is not resulting in reproduction. Maybe more plainly put, wherever you find a Christian who is not leading men and women to Christ, something is not right.

To be a disciple of Jesus is to make disciples of Jesus. As I hope we've seen, this has been true ever since the first century when Jesus invited four men to follow him. His words have echoed throughout this book: "Follow me, and I will make you fishers of men."[3] More important than searching for fish all over the sea, these men would spread the gospel all over the world. They would give their lives not simply to being disciples of Jesus, but sacrificially to making disciples of Jesus. And God's design for twenty-first-century disciples is exactly the same. Jesus calls every one of his disciples to make disciples who make disciples until the gospel penetrates every group of people in the world.

But something is wrong. Very wrong. Somewhere along the way, we have lost sight of what it means to be a disciple, and we have laid aside Jesus' command to make disciples. We have tragically minimized what it means to be his follower, and we have virtually ignored the biblical expectation that we fish for men. The result is a rampant spectator mentality that skews discipleship across the church, stifles the spread of the gospel around the world, and ultimately sears the heart of what it means for each of us to be a Christian.

A PERSONAL DISCIPLE-MAKING PLAN

This book represents an admittedly feeble attempt to address a malady in contemporary Christianity. While multitudes of men and women often loosely and many times falsely claim to be Christians, I have sought to explore what it actually means to follow Jesus. Becoming a Christian involves responding to the gracious invitation of God in Christ, and being a Christian involves leaving behind superficial religion for supernatural regeneration. As we follow Christ, he transforms our minds, our desires, our wills, our relationships, and our ultimate reason for living. Every disciple of Jesus exists to make disciples of Jesus, here and among every people group on the planet. There are no spectators. We are all born to reproduce.

So are you reproducing? To quote Dawson Trotman, "Men, where is your man? Women, where is your woman? Where is the one whom you led to Christ and who is now going on with

Him? . . . How many persons do you know by name today who were won to Christ by you and are now living for Him?"[4]

My purpose in asking these questions is not to make you feel guilty if you cannot answer them (or proud if you can). My purpose in asking these questions is to spur you on to consider how the life of Christ *in* you might be multiplied *through* you in the world.

Maybe a more important first question, though, is this: Do you desire to reproduce? Deep down inside, do you long to see people come to know Christ through your life? If the answer to that question is not an unhesitating, unapologetic yes, then I encourage you to search your heart. Is Christ in you? Do you believe his Word—his Word that claims that Christ alone is able to save sinners, that God alone is worthy of worship, and that all who do not receive God's grace in Christ will spend eternity in hell? Are you experiencing his affections—delight in knowing him and a desire to proclaim him to the people around you? Ultimately, are you abandoned to his will for you to be his witness in the world?

If these things are not a reality in your life, then no matter what decision you made however many years ago and no matter what church you attended last week, you may not actually be a Christian, for these features are the fruit of followers of Christ. If you don't desire to reproduce and if you don't long to see people come to know Christ through your life, then I encourage you, in the words of 2 Corinthians 13:5, to "examine [yourself] to see whether you are in the faith." Is Christ in you? And if he is not— if your heart, mind, and will have not been transformed by the forgiveness of your sins and the filling of his Spirit—then I urge you to die to sin and yourself today and come to life in Christ.

On the other hand, if you do desire to reproduce as a disciple of Jesus, and if you do long to see people come to know Christ through your life, then I invite you to take some intentional steps toward that end. Every year, I fill out what I call a "personal disciple-making plan." Basically, it's my effort in God's grace to set out how I want to wholeheartedly follow Christ and fish for men in the coming year. Each of the pastors in our church writes out a similar plan, and every new member of our church goes through the same process. My prayer is that every follower of Christ in the church I have the privilege of pastoring would have an intentional plan for following Jesus and fishing for men.

Consequently, as this book comes to a close, I want to invite you to walk through a similar process of writing out a specific plan for how you are going to follow Jesus and fish for men. If the end result of reading this book is only a slightly clearer understanding of what it means to be a disciple, then these pages will have been for the most part wasted. But if the end result of reading this book is a significantly greater understanding of what it means for you to be a disciple that inevitably leads you to make disciples here and around the world, then these pages will have proven, I pray, eternally valuable.

So for every follower of Christ, I invite you to consider the following six straightforward questions. Pages have been provided for you to write out your plan here in the book, but feel free to record your commitment in whatever way works best for you. I have tried to keep the primary questions simple, yet I have also provided additional questions that might help you flesh out what it means to follow Jesus in each of these ways. I don't presume that these questions are exhaustive, but I do believe they are essential. And my hope and prayer is that they will serve you as you consider what it means to follow Christ.

1. HOW WILL I FILL MY MIND WITH TRUTH?

To follow Jesus is to believe Jesus, and in order to believe Jesus, we must listen to Jesus. The life of the disciple is the life of a learner. We constantly attune our ears to the words of our Master. As he teaches us through his Word, he transforms us in the world.

As disciples of Jesus, then, you and I must be intentional about filling our minds with his truth. In the words of Paul, "Whatever is true, whatever is noble, whatever is right, whatever is pure, whatever is lovely, whatever is admirable—if anything is excellent or praiseworthy—think about such things."[5] In the process of setting our minds on godly things, we guard our minds from worldly thinking. And the more we hear and know Christ through his Word, the more we will enjoy and honor Christ in the world.

So take time to consider how you will intentionally fill your mind with his truth. Specifically, ask the following questions:

- **How will I read God's Word?** You might start with a plan to read a chapter a day, and maybe that plan will increase to two, three, four, or more chapters a day. You might consider using an intentional Bible reading plan that covers all of Scripture over a certain period of time.[6] If the Bible is the revelation of God's Word to God's children, shouldn't every Christian actually read the whole thing?

- **How will I memorize God's Word?** As you read, look for verses, paragraphs, or even chapters that seem particularly significant and applicable to your life. Then commit them to memory. Again, maybe you can start by memorizing a verse a week, and then you can take on more as your hunger for hiding God's Word in your heart increases.

- **How will I learn God's Word from others?** Reading, studying, and understanding the Bible is not just an individual effort; it's a community project. As we saw in chapter 7, we all need pastors (including myself as I serve as a pastor!) who are teaching God's Word faithfully to us. And we all need brothers and sisters who are consistently encouraging us with God's Word. So as a member of a church and in your life as a Christian, what is your plan for consistently learning God's Word from and with others?

As you consider a plan for reading, memorizing, and learning God's Word, don't forget that disciples do these things not for information, but for transformation. As *believers in* Jesus, we are *followers of* Jesus, which means that we not only *hear* the truth of Christ; we *apply* the truth of Christ. Our goal as disciples is never just to believe God's Word; our goal is to obey God's Word. So as you plan to fill your mind with truth, purpose to follow the one who is Truth.

2. HOW WILL I FUEL MY AFFECTIONS FOR GOD?

Even as I encourage you to ask and answer these questions, I am mindful of the dangerous tendency for discipline in the disciple's life to become mechanical and monotonous. Our aim is not simply to know God; our aim is to love God, and the more we read his Word, the more we delight in his glory.

Our aim in other spiritual disciplines is similar. As we worship, pray, fast, and give, we fuel affection for God. So I want to encourage you to intentionally plan according to questions like these:

- **How will I worship?** Biblical passages like Romans 12:1 and 1 Corinthians 10:31 remind us that all of life is worship. To the church at Rome, Paul wrote, "I urge you, brothers, in view of God's mercy, to offer your bodies as living sacrifices, holy and pleasing to God—this is your spiritual act of worship."[7] To the church at Corinth, Paul said, "Whether you eat or drink or whatever you do, do it all for the glory of God."[8] So consider general ways that you might focus on worship in every facet of your life. Then, in light of Scripture's clear exhortation to meet regularly with the church for worship,[9] plan to gather with brothers and sisters weekly to express collective want for God through worship.

- **How will I pray?** Jesus said, "When you pray, go into your room and shut the door and pray to your Father who is in secret."[10] In other words, find yourself a place and set aside a time to be with the Father. You may wonder, *Doesn't Scripture teach us to pray all the time?* God's Word most definitely does say this in 1 Thessalonians 5:17, but I know in my own life that concentrated prayer at a specific time is the best fuel for continual prayer all the time. So what will be your time and where will be your place for communion with your Father? Simply setting aside this time and place will substantially change your life as a disciple of Jesus.

- **How will I fast?** The very idea of fasting may be altogether new to you, but Jesus' words to his disciples seem to imply that they will regularly set aside food in order to feast on God alone.[11] So if you've never fasted before, I encourage you to start by setting aside one meal. Once a week or once every few weeks, instead of eating breakfast, lunch, or dinner, spend that hour praying and reading God's Word. Once you've grown accustomed to this practice and discovered the value of this time (and an hour alone with God will quickly prove quite fulfilling), plan to fast for two meals in one day, and then for an entire twenty-four-hour period. As you grow in fasting, you may consider fasting for consecutive days on a periodic basis. Regardless, plan to fast from food so that you might learn to feast on God.

- **How will I give?** When you think about fueling affection for God, giving may not be the first thing that comes to your mind. But Jesus' teaching on giving in Scripture is directly associated with his teaching on fasting and prayer.

Immediately after he teaches his disciples about giving, praying, and then fasting, he says, "Do not store up for yourselves treasures on earth . . . but store up for yourselves treasures in heaven. . . . For where your treasure is, there your heart will be also."[12] Notice the tie between our money and our affections. According to Jesus, our money doesn't just reflect our hearts; our hearts follow our money. One of the most effective ways to fuel affection for God is to give your resources in obedience to God. So as a disciple of Jesus, how will you intentionally, generously, sacrificially, and cheerfully give to the church and to those in need around you and around the world? Such giving fuels selfless love for God that overcomes selfish desires for the things of this world.

Following Jesus involves not only intellectual trust in him, but also emotional desire for him. We have seen that it is impossible to separate true faith in Christ from profound feelings for Christ. So as disciples of Jesus, we intentionally worship, pray, fast, and give in order to fuel affection for God.

3. HOW WILL I SHARE GOD'S LOVE AS A WITNESS IN THE WORLD?

God's will in the world and for our lives is to spread his gospel, grace, and glory to all peoples. Instead of asking what God's will is for our lives, every disciple of Jesus asks, "How can my life align with his will for me to be his witness in the world?" This general question leads us to more specific questions.

- **Who?** You may remember Matthew from chapter 6, a member of the church I pastor who used to live in a Muslim country. If you recall, when men and women come to faith in Christ in that country, they immediately create a list of people they know and then commit to share the gospel with whoever is least likely to kill them. Now it's probable that if you're reading this book, you don't live in a country like that. Nevertheless, I want to give you the same challenge. You may not know a lot of people who will kill you because you're a Christian, but you are surrounded by people who are not Christians. So take a minute to write down the names of three, five, or maybe ten unbelievers God has placed in your life. Then begin praying specifically for God, through the power of his Spirit, to draw them to his salvation.

- **How?** You and I have opportunities to share the gospel every single day. In chapter 8, I described how Mark, Kim, and Robert are constantly sewing gospel threads into the fabric of their everyday conversations. So how can you do the same? In the context of where you live, work, and play, and with the people God has put around you (including the names of those you listed above), how can you begin to speak intentionally about God's character, man's sin, Christ's provision, and our need to respond to that provision? Would you commit to praying every single morning for grace to sew gospel threads all day long? Could you then look intentionally throughout the day for opportunities to share gospel truths, being ever attentive to situations that God might open for you to share the entire gospel and invite someone to trust in Christ?

- **When?** Instead of passively sitting back and waiting for people to ask you about Jesus, it's wise to consider how you can actively show Christ's love by creating opportunities to tell people about Jesus. Think particularly here about the people you identified above. How can you specifically and deliberately create opportunities to share the gospel with them? Could you invite them to lunch? Could you have them over for dinner? Is there some other activity or avenue you could take advantage of, whether that's something as involved as spending a day or weekend with them or something as simple as writing a letter to them?

As you identify the *who*, think through the *how*, and plan the *when*, don't forget the *why*. All of this can seem fabricated and fake until you remember what's at stake. Every person that God has graciously put around you is a sinner eternally in need of a Savior. You were once that person, yet someone intentionally sought you out to share the gospel with you. Now this is the purpose for which God has graciously saved you. So with the Word of God in your mouth and the Spirit of God in your heart, end your quest to find God's will by deciding today to follow it.

4. HOW WILL I SHOW GOD'S LOVE AS A MEMBER OF A CHURCH?

The Bible flies in the face of American individualism and church consumerism, prompting every follower of Christ to ask the question, *Am I an active, accountable member of a local church?* This question is not, *Is my name on a church roll somewhere?* or *Do I attend church somewhere?* The question is, *Am I committed to a local church where I am sharing life with other followers of Christ in mutual accountability under biblical leadership for the glory of God?* If not, the first question we need to ask is:

- **Where?** Throughout the year, the church I pastor hosts a four-week class for potential church members. During that time, I always say to every person in the class, "Is this the local body of Christ where you can most effectively make disciples of Christ?" If the answer to that question is yes, then I encourage them to lock arms with our local church, not as spectators on the sidelines, but as participants in the mission. If the answer to that question is no, then I encourage them to lock arms with another local church, where they can more effectively carry out the commission of Christ. So where is the place that you can most effectively make disciples of all nations? Where are the pastors you can follow confidently because they teach and model God's Word clearly? Where are the people you are going to serve and submit to as a disciple of Jesus?

Answering these questions and committing your life to a church then leads to another question.

- **What?** As you look across the church of which you are a member, consider what things you can do to build up (and be built up by) that body of Christ. Are there certain people you can serve in specific ways? Are there certain positions you can fill for specific purposes? What will you do to lay down your life for the people of that church? And what will you do to make sure that you have people who are watching out for your life in Christ, willing to pull you back whenever you start to wander from him?

To follow Christ is to love his church. It is biblically, spiritually, and practically impossible to be a disciple of Christ (much less make disciples of Christ) apart from total devotion to a family of Christians. So how will your life be spent showing God's love as a member of a church?

5. HOW WILL I SPREAD GOD'S GLORY AMONG ALL PEOPLES?

The eternal purpose of God is to save people through Christ. The clear commission of Christ for every single disciple is to make disciples not just generally, but of all nations—every *ethne* in the world. So regardless of where you live, how is your life going to impact every nation, tribe, tongue, and people in the world? This is not a question for extraordinary missionaries; this is a question for ordinary disciples. Consider the following ways you can play a part in the spread of God's glory to the ends of the earth.

- **How will I pray for the nations?** You and I have an opportunity to be a part of what God is doing around the world from our knees in our homes. So let's pray passionately for God's Kingdom to come and will to be done across the earth. You might use a tool like *Operation World* (available for free online unless you want a digital or hard copy) to pray for every nation in the world. Plan to deliberately focus your praying generally on the nations and specifically on the unreached people groups of the world.

- **How will I give to the nations?** In chapter 8, I mentioned how five cents of every one hundred dollars in a North American Christian's life goes through the church to the rest of the world. Plan to change that. How will you sacrifice the wants in your budget to give to the needs of the world—most particularly the need for every people group to hear the gospel? As a member of a church, how will you lead your church to cut programs and priorities that you once thought were important yet pale in comparison to the physical needs of starving brothers and sisters and the spiritual needs of unreached men and women all over the world? Plan to sacrifice and spend for the sake of the nations.

- **How will I go to the nations?** Strategically, creatively, and wisely consider ways you can share the gospel with other people groups, particularly those that are unreached (meaning they have no access to the gospel). Some of these people groups have come to America and may be in your community, so consider ways you might reach out to them, whether they're Somali Muslims, Egyptian Arabs, Tibetan Buddhists, or any other people group right around you. Then consider ways you might cross the ocean to go to them, whether that's on a short-term trip for a week or two, a mid-term endeavor for a year or two, or a long-term commitment for a decade or two. Consider all the avenues in which you might spend your life, lead your family, or leverage your work to penetrate the people groups of the world with the gospel, for this is what you were created for.

In the church I pastor, we continually refer to what we call the "blank check." As followers of Christ, we have given him a "blank check" with our lives, meaning that we are his to spend for the spread of the gospel in the world. Our time is his, our money is his, our families are his, and our future is his. No strings attached. We want to go wherever he leads, give whatever he requires, and obey whatever he commands. Every time we sense God leading us as a church toward another unreached people group, we ask everyone in the church to put the "blank check" back on the table and ask God if he wants them to go.

So does God have a "blank check" with your life? Have you laid everything on the table and asked him, *How do you want me (or my family) to give to the nations?* Have you asked him, *How do you want me (or my family) to go to the nations? Do you want us to move overseas for the spread of your fame?* In prayer, as you put these questions before God, I am confident that he will answer clearly. As we've seen, he wants his will to be accomplished through us more than we do. And as we follow him, he will lead us to the people, places, and positions where we can most effectively make disciples of all nations for the glory of his name.

6. HOW WILL I MAKE DISCIPLE MAKERS AMONG A FEW PEOPLE?

Asking the above questions about the nations can feel overwhelming. Can we realistically be a part of the spread of the gospel to every people group on the planet? The answer to that question, though, is surprisingly simple.

Think about it. Of all the men and women who have ever lived on the earth, Jesus was the most passionate about the spread of God's glory to all peoples. And what did he do? He spent his life investing in a few people. His strategy for reaching all peoples was clear: make disciple makers among a few people.

As we've seen, God will lead us to live in all kinds of different places in the world. Yet regardless of where we live, the task we have is the same. Whether you're a pastor who leads a church or a mother who works at home, and whether you're in the mountains of northern Afghanistan or the plains of midwestern America, God has commanded every disciple to make disciples. No Christian is excused from this command, and no Christian would want to escape this command. So every one of us looks around and asks,

How will I make disciple makers among a few people? This question naturally breaks down into others:

- **How will I bring them in?** Making disciple makers starts with identifying a small group of men or women (depending, of course, on your gender, assuming that disciple making is best done with men together or women together). Consider two, three, or four people God has put in your sphere of influence whom you can lead to make disciples. Ask God for the names of specific people, or if you're having trouble, ask a pastor or leader in your church for help. Then invite those few people to spend intentional time with you in the days ahead for the express purpose of growing in Christ together.

- **How will I teach them to obey?** As we've seen, disciple making involves teaching people to obey everything Christ has commanded us. So think through how this will happen with the few people your life is focused on. What do you need to teach them from God's Word? How can you teach them in a way that helps them learn to read and understand God's Word themselves? Maybe you read through a Bible book together, or maybe you use some other tool for Bible study. Regardless of what you do, though, don't settle for simply teaching them information. Focus on seeing their transformation. When you gather together, ask questions about how they are following Christ and fishing for men. You might start by using the six questions here to lead them to develop their own plans for being and making disciples. These questions could then become a basis for you to ask them (and them to ask you) how they are following Jesus and whom they are telling about Jesus. As we've seen, grace-saturated, gospel-driven mutual accountability like this is absolutely essential to being disciples and making disciples.

- **How will I model obedience?** This is where disciple making gets both interesting and invigorating. We have seen in Matthew 4 that Jesus has called us to follow him. Yet once we do this, and we begin fishing for men, we find ourselves in a position where we are now leading other people to follow us. Paul virtually said to the Corinthian Christians, "Follow me as I follow Christ."[13] He told the Philippian Christians, "Whatever you have learned or received or heard from me, or seen in me—put it into practice. And the God of peace will be with you."[14] Paul had so lived his life in front of these believers that he could say, "Follow my example." Now that certainly didn't mean he was perfect, and we definitely don't have to be perfect in order to make disciples. But as you focus your life on the few people God has given you, they need to see and hear and sense the life of Christ in you. So invite them into your home. Let them see you with your family. Show them how to pray, study the Bible, and share the gospel. Practically, making disciple makers involves looking at these few people and saying to them: "Follow me." So plan intentional ways to model what it means to follow Christ.

- **How will I send them out?** As you teach the commands of Christ and model the life of Christ, one of the commands you are teaching and modeling is Jesus' command to make disciples. The goal is not just for these few people you are focused on to follow Jesus; the goal is for them to fish for men. So the time comes when you commission those few to find a few people of their own. By then you have shown them what it means to make disciples, so now you send them out to do the same. Of course, you continue to encourage, serve, teach, care for, and pray for them, but you also release them to take the time they have spent with you and begin to spend it with others doing the same thing you have done. In this way, your life literally begins to multiply the gospel in the world through disciples you have made.

  Francis Chan and I have developed material called "Multiply" for the purpose of practically helping disciples to make disciple makers. This material is available for free online at www.multiplymovement.com. Regardless of whether you use this material, another resource, or simply God's Word, the goal is the same: decide to spend your life making disciple makers among a few people.

THE KING'S CALL

This was Jesus' strategy for bringing the Good News of God's grace and glory to all the world. Two thousand years ago, he wandered the streets and byways of Israel. He was initiating a revolution, but his revolution didn't revolve around the masses or multitudes.

It revolved around a few men. Those few disciples would learn to think like him, love like him, teach like him, live like him, and serve like him. As he transformed followers, they became fishers, and you and I have the gospel today because they were faithful in making disciple makers.

So let us be faithful to do the same. We are followers of Jesus. We have died to ourselves, and we now live in Christ. He has saved us from our sins and has satisfied our souls. He has transformed our minds with his truth, fulfilled our desires with his joy, and conformed our ways to his will. He has joined us together in bodies of believers called local churches for the accomplishment of one all-consuming commission: the declaration of his gospel and the display of his glory to all the peoples of the world.

This task involves all of us. No child of God is intended by God to be sidelined as a spectator in the great commission. Every child of God has been invited by God to be on the front lines of the supreme mission in all of history. Every disciple of Jesus has been called, loved, created, and saved to make disciples of Jesus who make disciples of Jesus who make disciples of Jesus until the grace of God is enjoyed and the glory of God is exalted among every people group on the planet. And on that day, every disciple of Jesus—every follower of Christ and fisher of men—will see the Savior's face and behold the Father's splendor in a scene of indescribable beauty and everlasting bliss that will never, ever fade away.

This is a call worth dying for.

This is a King worth living for.

A PERSONAL
DISCIPLE-MAKING PLAN

Record here your answers to the questions raised in chapter 9, "BORN TO REPRODUCE."

---

1. HOW WILL I FILL MY MIND WITH TRUTH?

_____

_____

_____

_____

How will I read God's Word? _(See pages 211–212.)_

_____

_____

_____

_____

How will I memorize God's Word? *(See page 212.)*

_____

_____

_____

_____

How will I learn God's Word from others? *(See page 212.)*

_____

_____

_____

_____

2. HOW WILL I FUEL MY AFFECTIONS FOR GOD?

_____

_____

_____

_____

How will I worship? *(See page 213.)*

_____

_____

_____

_____

How will I pray? *(See pages 213–214.)*

_____

_____

_____

_____

_____

How will I fast? *(See page 214.)*

_____

_____

_____

_____

How will I give? *(See pages 214–215.)*

_____

_____

_____

_____

3. HOW WILL I SHARE GOD'S LOVE AS A WITNESS IN THE WORLD?

_____

_____

_____

_____

Who? *(See page 216.)*

_____

_____

_____

_____

How? *(See pages 216–217.)*

_____

_____

_____

_____

When? *(See page 217.)*

_____

_____

_____

_____

4. HOW WILL I SHOW GOD'S LOVE AS A MEMBER OF A CHURCH?

_____

_____

_____

_____

Where? *(See page 218.)*

_____

_____

_____

_____

What? *(See page 219.)*

_____

_____

_____

_____

---

5. HOW WILL I SPREAD GOD'S GLORY AMONG ALL PEOPLES?

_____

_____

_____

_____

How will I pray for the nations? *(See page 220.)*

_____

_____

_____

_____

How will I give to the nations? *(See page 220.)*

_____
_____
_____
_____

How will I go to the nations? *(See pages 220–221.)*

_____
_____
_____
_____

6. HOW WILL I MAKE DISCIPLE MAKERS AMONG A FEW PEOPLE?

_____
_____
_____
_____

How will I bring them in? *(See page 223.)*

_____
_____
_____
_____

How will I teach them to obey? *(See pages 223–224.)*

_____

_____

_____

_____

How will I model obedience? *(See page 224.)*

_____

_____

_____

_____

How will I send them out? *(See page 225.)*

_____

_____

_____

_____

ACKNOWLEDGMENTS

As I consider the measure of grace necessary to make this book a reality, I am grateful to God for many people on many levels.

I am grateful to God for the entire team at Tyndale, and particularly for Ron and Lisa, whose encouragement to me, patience with me, and belief in me have far exceeded what I deserve.

I am grateful to God for Sealy, without whose tireless work and trusted friendship I would be lost in this process.

I am grateful to God for the *Radical* crew—for Jim's selfless leadership, for Cory's faithful support, for Angelia's passionate service, for David's gracious wisdom, and for the humble dedication of every person on this team.

I am grateful to God for the people in my life who have shown me most personally and powerfully what it means to be a disciple of Jesus and to make disciples of Jesus. Whether it's partners in ministry like Francis, mentors in ministry like Jim and Mark, or men around the world like Anil and Hari, their impact in my life cannot be overestimated.

I am grateful to God for the elders, staff, and members of The Church at Brook Hills. I still can't believe these brothers and sisters allow me to shepherd them. This work is the fruit of our faith family as we give our lives together for the accomplishment of the great commission.

I am grateful to God for my family. Simply put, they have sacrificed the most to make this book a reality. I have written this book particularly in honor of my four children, yet they and I both know that their mom is the real hero in our home. I am grateful to God for Heather, my beautiful bride whose love for Christ shines most brightly in her love, support, service, encouragement, and care for me. I am blessed beyond words.

More than anything, I am grateful to God for his great invitation to be a disciple of Jesus. I shudder to think of where I would be apart from his grace in the gospel. My singular prayer is that such grace toward me might be to great effect for him (John 3:30).

NOTES

INTRODUCTION

1. John 10:10, ESV
2. 2 Timothy 2:4, ESV
3. See 1 Corinthians 10:13.
4. See Philippians 2:12-13; 4:13, 19.
5. See Ephesians 2:10.
6. Matthew 28:18-20, ESV
7. Rodney Stark, *Cities of God* (New York: HarperCollins, 2006), 67.
8. *Asian Report* 197 (Oct/Nov 1992), 9.
9. Matthew 11:30
10. Matthew 28:20, ESV
11. See Acts 1:8.
12. See Luke 18–19.
13. 2 Corinthians 7:10, ESV
14. Acts 20:26-27, ESV
15. 2 Timothy 4:6-8, ESV
16. John 17:4, ESV
17. Matthew 10:32-33, ESV

CHAPTER 1: UNCONVERTED BELIEVERS

1. Matthew 4:19
2. Matthew 7:21-23
3. Galatians 2:20, ESV
4. Matthew 7:13-14, ESV
5. Matthew 10:17-22
6. Matthew 16:16, 24-25
7. Matthew 24:9
8. Oswald Chambers, *My Utmost for His Highest*, entry for May 30, accessed at www.utmost.org.

9. Luke 14:26-27, 33
10. John 3:16; Acts 16:31; Romans 10:9, emphasis mine
11. James 2:19
12. Matthew 7:21
13. Barna Group, "Barna Study of Religious Change Since 1991 Shows Significant Changes by Faith Group," August 4, 2011; Barna Group, "Most American Christians Do Not Believe that Satan or the Holy Spirit Exist," April 10, 2009.
14. I first heard a version of this illustration years ago in a recorded sermon by Paul Washer.
15. From the "Jamaica" entry in *Operation World: The Definitive Prayer Guide to Every Nation*, http://www.operationworld.org/jama.
16. See 2 Corinthians 4:4.
17. See Matthew 4:17.
18. See Matthew 3:2.
19. Acts 2:37-38
20. Ezekiel 14:6
21. See 1 Thessalonians 1:9-10.
22. The opposite is actually true, for unlike the unbeliever, the Christian fights a continual battle to turn aside from the idolatry and immorality of this world. Such ongoing repentance in the daily Christian life is the overflow of initial repentance at the beginning of the Christian life. This dynamic will be explored more in the pages to come.
23. Galatians 2:20

CHAPTER 2: THE GREAT INVITATION

1. See Genesis 6:5; 8:21.
2. See Genesis 19.
3. See Numbers 15.
4. See Joshua 7.
5. See Leviticus 10.
6. See 2 Samuel 6.
7. See Colossians 1:21.
8. See John 8:34; 2 Timothy 2:26.
9. See John 3:20; Ephesians 4:18.
10. See Romans 6:19.
11. See Romans 1:28; 2 Corinthians 4:4.
12. See Romans 1:26; 1 Peter 2:11.
13. See Romans 1:24; Genesis 8:21; Matthew 9:12.
14. Romans 3:10-18
15. Ephesians 2:1-2
16. Deuteronomy 7:7-8
17. Jeremiah 1:5
18. John 15:16
19. See Matthew 1–4.

20. Matthew 3:17
21. Matthew 4:19
22. Greg Garrison, "Birmingham's Church at Brook Hills Pastor Pens Book Telling Christians to Avoid Worldly Wealth," *The Birmingham News*, June 12, 2010.
23. Isaiah 53:5-6, emphasis mine
24. Isaiah 53:6
25. Ephesians 1:3-6
26. See Luke 15:1-7.

CHAPTER 3: SUPERFICIAL RELIGION AND SUPERNATURAL REGENERATION

1. John 14:6, emphasis mine
2. John MacArthur, *Matthew 8–15*, vol. 2 in *The MacArthur New Testament Commentary* (Chicago: Moody Publishers, 1987), 282.
3. Matthew 11:28-29
4. W. Ian Thomas, *The Saving Life of Christ and the Mystery of Godliness* (Grand Rapids: Zondervan, 1988), 181.
5. Ibid., 101, 85.
6. John 3:3, 5
7. Ezekiel 36:25-28
8. Jeremiah 31:33-34
9. Matthew 1:21
10. John 1:29
11. Isaiah 1:18
12. Psalm 51:2
13. 1 Corinthians 6:11
14. 1 John 1:9, ESV
15. Titus 3:4-5
16. Matthew 9:2
17. 1 Corinthians 15:55-57
18. Ezekiel 36:26-27, emphasis mine
19. See Galatians 2:20.
20. Romans 8:10-11
21. Matthew 4:19, emphasis mine
22. Matthew 28:19-20

CHAPTER 4: DON'T MAKE JESUS YOUR PERSONAL LORD AND SAVIOR

1. Philippians 2:10-11
2. Barna Group, "Most American Christians Do Not Believe That Satan or the Holy Spirit Exist," April 10, 2009.
3. See James 2:19.
4. John 14:17, 26, ESV
5. John 8:31-32, ESV
6. John 15:7, ESV
7. See 1 Corinthians 2:16.

8. See Romans 12:2.

9. Colossians 3:9-10, ESV

10. 2 Corinthians 10:5

11. Blaise Pascal, *Pensées*, section 592. In addition, Gary Habermas, probably the most renowned contemporary scholar on the resurrection of Jesus, who has studied volumes of research on the Resurrection and has debated numerous scholars on each side of this issue, concludes, "When the early and eyewitness experiences of the disciples, James, and Paul are considered, along with their corresponding transformations and their central message, the historical resurrection of Jesus becomes the only plausible explanation of the facts." At the end of N. T. Wright's exhaustive treatise on the Resurrection, he writes, "The early Christians did not invent the empty tomb and the meetings or sightings of the risen Jesus. Nobody was expecting this kind of thing. No kind of conversion experience would have invented it. To suggest otherwise is to stop doing history and enter into a fantasy world of our own."

12. John 5:22-24, 26-29

13. Revelation 20:11-15

14. James Denney and Alexander Maclaren, *The Epistles of St. Paul to the Colossians and Philemon*, Expositor's Bible, vol. 31 (New York: Armstrong, 1905), 300.

15. Genesis 3:1

16. See Luke 16:22-23; Matthew 22:13.

17. See 2 Thessalonians 1:9.

18. See Matthew 25:46.

19. Richard Hofstadter, *America at 1750: A Social Portrait*, Vintage International Vintage Series (New York: Vintage, 1973), 240.

20. John 11:25-26

21. John 3:16

22. John 14:1-6

23. Revelation 21:1, 4

24. Philippians 1:21

25. See Galatians 2:20.

26. Luke 24:47

27. Revelation 5:9

28. John 15:7, ESV

29. Daniel 7:14, ESV

30. Matthew 28:18-19

31. Ephesians 1:20-21

32. John 14:6

33. John 3:16, 18

CHAPTER 5: CHILDREN OF GOD

1. Matthew 6:9

2. J. I. Packer, *Knowing God* (Downers Grove: InterVarsity Press, 1973), 200–201.

3. John Wesley, *The Journal of the Reverend John Wesley*, January 29, 1738.

4. See: for forgiving, Matthew 6:11-15; for providing, Matthew 6:25-33; for leading, Romans 8:14; for protecting, Romans 8:15; for sustaining, 1 Corinthians 8:6; for comforting, 2 Corinthians 1:3; for directing, 1 Thessalonians 3:11; for purifying, 1 Thessalonians 3:13; for disciplining, Hebrews 12:5-11; for giving to, James 1:17; for calling, Jude 1:1; for promising his inheritance, Colossians 1:12.
5. Jonathan Edwards, *Religious Affections*, abridged and updated by Ellyn Sanna (Uhrichsville, OH: Barbour Publishing, 1999), 46–48.
6. John 6:35
7. See Genesis 2:16.
8. Genesis 3:6
9. See Exodus 16; Deuteronomy 8:3.
10. John 6:32
11. John 6:34
12. John 6:35, emphasis mine
13. John 6:33
14. C. S. Lewis, "The Weight of Glory," in *The Weight of Glory: And Other Addresses* (New York: HarperCollins, 2001), 26.
15. Psalm 19:8, 10-11
16. Psalm 119:14, 20, 24, 47, 97, 111, 131, 162, 167
17. Matthew 4:4, quoting Deuteronomy 8:3
18. Matthew 6:8
19. Matthew 6:6
20. Matthew 6:6
21. Psalm 63:1, 5-6
22. Ezra 9:6
23. C. S. Lewis, *Reflections on the Psalms* (Orlando: Harcourt, 1986), 94–95.
24. See Matthew 6:9-18.
25. 2 Corinthians 8:9
26. 2 Corinthians 9:7

CHAPTER 6: GOD'S WILL FOR YOUR LIFE

1. Matthew 4:19
2. The titles for these methods of finding God's will are not my own. I have seen them in a variety of different sources and adapted them for use here.
3. Galatians 2:20
4. Romans 6:3-4
5. Oswald Chambers, *My Utmost for His Highest*, entry for March 20 (classic edition), accessed at www.utmost.org.
6. See Genesis 1:26-28.
7. See Genesis 12:1-3; 26:4; 28:14.
8. Psalm 67:1-2
9. Isaiah 66:18-19, ESV
10. Habakkuk 2:14
11. See Matthew 28:18-20; Luke 24:47-49; Acts 1:8.

12. Romans 15:8-9
13. Romans 15:20-21
14. 2 Peter 3:9, NKJV
15. Luke 19:10
16. See John 17:18.
17. Matthew 28:19
18. See John 4:24; 6:63; 14:15-17, 25-26; 15:26-27; 16:4-15; 1 Corinthians 2:6-16; 12:1-11; Galatians 5:22-23.
19. Acts 1:8
20. Matthew 28:19; Luke 24:47-48
21. Numbers 11:25
22. Numbers 24:2-3
23. 2 Samuel 23:2, ESV
24. 2 Chronicles 24:20
25. Nehemiah 9:30
26. Ezekiel 11:5
27. Luke 1:15-16
28. Luke 1:41-42
29. Luke 1:67
30. Acts 2:4
31. Acts 4:8
32. Acts 4:31
33. Acts 9:17-20
34. Acts 13:9-10
35. The only one that's not directly clear about this is Luke 1:15-16, but remember that this was a prophecy about John the Baptist, the forerunner of Christ, whose purpose in redemptive history was to verbally proclaim the coming of the Kingdom of God.
36. See Acts 2:33, 47; 9:1-31; 10:1-48; 13:1-4; 16:6-10, 14.
37. Psalm 34:8, ESV

CHAPTER 7: THE BODY OF CHRIST

1. Acts 9:4
2. See 1 Corinthians 10:16; 2 Corinthians 13:14; Philippians 1:5; 3:10; and 1 John 1:3-7, respectively.
3. See: for caring, 1 Corinthians 12:25; loving, John 13:34-35; hosting, 1 Peter 4:9; receiving, Romans 15:7; honoring, Romans 12:10; serving, Galatians 5:13; instructing, Romans 15:14; forgiving, Colossians 3:13; motivating, Hebrews 10:24; building up, 1 Thessalonians 5:13; encouraging, 1 Thessalonians 5:11; comforting, 2 Corinthians 1:3-7; praying for and confessing sin to, James 5:16; esteeming, Philippians 2:3; edifying, Romans 14:19; teaching, Colossians 3:16; showing kindness to, Ephesians 4:32; giving to, Acts 2:45 and 2 Corinthians 8–9; weeping with, Romans 12:15; rejoicing with, 1 Corinthians 12:27; restoring, Galatians 6:1-5 and Matthew 18:15-20.

4. 1 Thessalonians 3:8, ESV
5. Philippians 4:1, ESV
6. Dietrich Bonhoeffer, *Life Together* (New York: Harper & Row, 1954), 107.
7. Dietrich Bonhoeffer, *The Cost of Discipleship* (New York: Touchstone, 1959), 288.
8. See especially Ezekiel 36:22-23; 1 Peter 2:9.
9. 1 Corinthians 12:12-27, ESV, emphasis mine
10. Ephesians 3:20-21
11. See Acts 11:22; 1 Corinthians 1:2; Galatians 1:2; and 1 Thessalonians 1:1 and 2 Thessalonians 1:1, respectively.
12. See Romans 16:5; Colossians 4:15; Philemon 1:2.
13. Matthew 18:15-17, ESV
14. 1 Corinthians 5:13
15. Hebrews 13:17
16. Mark 10:44
17. See Acts 20; 1 Timothy 3:1-13; Titus 1:5-9; 1 Peter 5:1-5.
18. John 13:34-35
19. John 17:20-21
20. Ephesians 3:10

CHAPTER 8: A VISION OF THE POSSIBLE

1. Matthew 4:19
2. Matthew 28:18-20
3. Romans 10:13
4. This is where books like 1 John biblically ground our assurance as believers.
5. 1 Thessalonians 1:5-6
6. See 1 Timothy 3:2; 5:17; James 3:1.
7. Deuteronomy 6:7-9
8. Revelation 7:9-10
9. Revelation 5:9
10. Matthew 6:9-10
11. Generous Giving, "Key Statistics on Generous Giving," http://library. generousgiving.org/page.asp?sec=4&page=311.
12. Steve Corbett and Brian Fikkert, *When Helping Hurts: How to Alleviate Poverty without Hurting the Poor . . . and Yourself* (Chicago: Moody Publishers, 2012), 41.
13. Psalm 67:6-7
14. See Acts 16:11-15.
15. William Danker, quoted in Ruth A. Tucker, *From Jerusalem to Irian Jaya: A Biographical History of Christian Missions* (Grand Rapids: Zondervan, 2004), 99.

CHAPTER 9: BORN TO REPRODUCE

1. Dawson Trotman, "Born to Reproduce," 5, 12. Retrieved from Discipleship Library, http://www.discipleshiplibrary.com/pdfs/AA094.pdf.
2. Ibid., 14, 10.
3. Matthew 4:19

4. Trotman, "Born to Reproduce," 13, 10.
5. Philippians 4:8
6. For different Bible reading plan options, see "Read through the Entire Word" under "Resources" at The Radical Experiment, http://www.radicalexperiment.org/resources.html.
7. Romans 12:1
8. 1 Corinthians 10:31
9. See Hebrews 10:24-25.
10. Matthew 6:6, ESV
11. See, for example, Matthew 6:16-18.
12. Matthew 6:19-21
13. See 1 Corinthians 11:1.
14. Philippians 4:9

ABOUT THE AUTHOR

DR. DAVID PLATT is the lead pastor of The Church at Brook Hills in Birmingham, Alabama. As the author of the *New York Times* bestselling book *Radical: Taking Back Your Faith from the American Dream*, David has traveled extensively around the world, teaching the Bible and training church leaders. A lifelong learner, David has earned two undergraduate and three advanced degrees. David and his wife, Heather, live in Alabama with their family.

What is Jesus worth to you?

"David Platt challenges Christians to wake up, trade in false values rooted in the American Dream, and embrace the notion that each of us is blessed by God for a global purpose...This is a must-read for every believer!"

—*Wess Stafford,*
President and CEO,
Compassion International

Radical is a daring call for Christians to believe and obey the gospel according to Jesus—even if it flies in the face of success according to the American church. David Platt reveals what can happen when we exchange our convenient beliefs for authentic discipleship.

Find information, tools for individual application, church resources, and video at **RadicalTheBook.com.**